Landmarks
FINLAND IN THE WORLD

MAUNO KOIVISTO

Landmarks
FINLAND IN THE WORLD

KIRJAYHTYMÄ · HELSINKI

Edited by
Keijo Immonen
Jaakko Kalela

Translated by
Gregory Coogan

ISBN 951-26-2802-3

Typeset by: Tammer-Linkki Oy, Tampere 1985

Printed and bound by Mäntän Kirjapaino Oy, Mänttä, 1985

Contents

Foreword

The President of Finland is constitutionally responsible for the conduct of relations with foreign countries. Before my election and on several occasions since, I have said that I consider my most important task to be that of ensuring that the foreign-policy line built up and staked out by my predecessors J.K. Paasikivi and Urho Kekkonen is adhered to.

This has not been a difficult task, because the Paasikivi-Kekkonen Line enjoys the support of the entire nation.

Foreign powers, too, have faith in the continuity of our foreign policy. This has been clearly evident in the discussions that I have had with senior representatives of both our close neighbours and other countries since the beginning of my term of office.

The starting point in our successful foreign policy has been Finland's ability to maintain good relations with her neighbours whatever the circumstances. That goal revolves around more than a political wisdom that has been known and recognized, with varying degrees of clarity, since the days of Machiavelli and expresses a principle

6

in which the most central lessons of our country's history are summed up.

When a nation, confident in its own abilities, is willing and able to live in harmony with its neighbours, it fulfills the preconditions for being able to contribute to safeguarding peace and development in broader international contexts as well.

One has to find a line between two extreme attitudes; it is inconceivable that only directly related aspects can be taken into consideration in arriving at each individual decision, but neither is it a good idea to look backwards all the time just to make sure that one is leaving a straight wake in steering towards future situations.

I have performed many tasks and held many positions in Finnish society. I have sometimes been very dissatisfied with that society, and with myself.

I am grateful for the fact that I have been able to devote myself to pondering theoretical questions when they have prompted my interest. When I had brought my view of the world into satisfactory order, and before it had lost its freshness, I became involved in practical societal decision making.

I succeeded in promoting the achievement of many things that I considered important, only to realize how unimportant they become once they have been achieved.

I have not been able to change the world much,

but the world has changed me; and, apparently, that change has not been for the better.

I was a dissident and a rebel, until I was put in charge of keeping order. Now I look askance at anybody who rocks the boat.

This book sets forth stances that I took on foreign-policy and international questions in 1979—85. It is not my intention to sketch a comprehensive picture of Finland's foreign policy, but rather to present a concise outline of my positions on key questions relating to our external relations. I hope that these pointers will prove useful to persons actively interested in foreign policy, both in Finland and abroad.

1. Historical Notes

Forty years ago, with the Second World War still raging elsewhere in Europe, Finland disengaged from the war by signing, on 19 September, 1944, the Moscow Armistice Agreement with the Soviet Union and Britain. This event meant the watershed between two distinct historical periods: the early decades of independence and the post-war period.

The advent of peace had been long and fervently awaited by the Finnish people. The flow of death notices was staunched, long-blacked-out lights came on again, and reconstruction could begin.

However, peace did not come like a bolt of lightning from the heavens. The development of the military situation had been more than clear and it was obvious that the war could not go on much longer. Fighting on the Finnish front had first ebbed and given way to a ceasefire. Many wild rumours continued to circulate even after the ceasefire had taken effect.

Publication of the terms of the armistice did much to cast light on the future fate of the nation. They were largely what had been expected, but also contained many new points which would be difficult to implement.

One thing, however, was clear: implementation of those terms, primarily the expulsion of German forces and later the payment of a war indemnity, was clearly within the bounds of possibility and would depend on the actions of Finland's national leaders and citizens. But what was of paramount importance was that trust be created in relations between our countries. And that would require a lot of effort.

The signing of the Armistice Agreement freed Finland's leaders from the problems of warfare, except for what was involved in expelling the Germans, and confronted them with new tasks.

A new foreign policy had to be built up on new points of departure. Lasting conciliation with the Soviet Union had to be accomplished.

There were also major changes to be made in domestic policy. Much of the old had to go and new forces had to emerge. Forces that had been discriminated against until then were allowed to participate in managing the country's affairs and seek popular support for their goals.

Although the events of autumn 1944 represented a major political watershed, they did not bring the kind of profound social upheaval that was experienced in other countries that had been involved in the war. Finland retained her traditional legal and social systems. The political leaders who bore the main responsibility for piloting our foreign policy onto a new course that autumn had begun their political careers when Finland was still an autonomous grand duchy within the Russian Empire and had continued to hold key posts during the early years of independence.

The cessation of hostilities placed many Finns

between two epochs, as it were; what had earlier been taken for granted was uncertain and frightening during this period of transition. These feelings were aptly described by Prime Minister Paasikivi in a radio speech to the people of Finland on Independence Day, 6 December, 1944.

In this historic speech, Paasikivi admitted that in the midst of pivotal events small states experience hesitation in finding the proper course. As he put it, many people in these new circumstances, "as though awakening from slumber, look gropingly at the world around them before they gradually become animated and notice what the new circumstances are like and what they require".

As Paasikivi saw it, the starting point for everything in this situation had to be recognition of realities. The most central of these facts, a question of fateful consequence to our foreign policy, was our relations with the Soviet Union. It was to that question that the Finns had to find a solution, on which the future of our people would depend. We would have to build up good relations with our great power neighbour in the East. Traditional suspicion had to be dispelled and trust created in its place.

But amidst all the gloom and pessimism then, factors that inspired faith in our future could also be seen. The Soviet Union and the other victor nations had in the Moscow Armistice Agreement demonstrated their willingness to forge relations

13

with an independent Finland. That created the preconditions for the creation of good neighbourly relations based on mutual trust. It was also natural to continue the broad range of contacts that we had had for centuries with the other Nordic countries, Sweden in particular.

On the basis of those auspicious preconditions, Paasikivi determinedly set about his task of building up Finland's future position in international politics. As things were then, the most important way to go about this was to meet the terms of the Armistice Agreement scrupulously and in full.

The new post-war foreign policy direction had not yet been worked out in autumn 1944. Only gradually did it develop into a consistent foreign policy line. An important milestone in this development was the normalization of Finland's international position with the Paris Peace Treaty of 1947.

The development that had begun after the war in Finland was confirmed in 1948, just under four years after the signing of the armistice, when the Fenno-Soviet Treaty of Friendship, Cooperation and Mutual Assistance was concluded. In the years since then, this document has demonstrated its historic importance. Taking the fundamental interests of both sides into consideration, it far-sightedly steered our relations with the East into new channels.

An excellent indication of the positive develop-

14

ment that had taken place in Fenno-Soviet relations was the return of the Porkkala base area, long before the expiry of the lease period, at the end of 1955. This event can be considered to mark the end of the period of construction in our relations with the East. Thus, when President Paasikivi was leaving office in the beginning of 1956, he could note that he had succeeded in his policy of accomplishing that atmosphere of trust in Fenno-Soviet relations to the inescapability of which he had referred on Independence Day in 1944.

On this basis, President Kekkonen began determinedly to strengthen and expand Fenno-Soviet relations. It was then that such valuable practices as meetings between leaders of both countries began to emerge. Economic, scientific, technological and cultural relations gradually acquired their present shape and scope. In addition to that, an extensive network of agreements covering a variety of fields was built up.

Co-operation arrangements and mechanisms that have subsequently been applied in relations between other market-economy countries and the Soviet Union also date from the Kekkonen era. Indeed, the principles enshrined in the Final Act of the Conference on Security and Co-operation in Europe (CSCE), signed in Helsinki in 1975, had already been applied in Fenno-Soviet relations long before that.

Our country's international position looked

weak in the autumn of 1944. It is not at all surprising that doubts and "doomsday forecasts" concerning our country's future were often presented both in Finland and beyond her borders in those days. Today, our position is both known and recognized. Since the end of the 1940s, our policy has been contributing to the maintenance of stable conditions in the Nordic region. In general, too, we have long been participating, as a fully-fledged member, in the work of the international community, having joined both the Nordic Council and the United Nations in 1955.

In accordance with our policy of neutrality, we have also rendered services to the international community in the promotion of security and peaceful solutions to problems. This work has included our active participation in the CSCE process and in efforts to achieve disarmament. We have also participated on a broad scale in UN peacekeeping operations and successfully offered our good offices in the arrangement of important international negotiations.

2. Fundamental Interests

Following several years of steady deterioration in the relations of the great powers, the turn of the present decade saw solutions that have brought in their wake a state of tension resembling that of the Cold War period. And it appears that this tension will be rather difficult to defuse. The arms race has been accelerating strongly and more and more new crisis spots are threatening world peace.

Crises outside Europe, such as the events in the Gulf region, inevitably affect our continent, too. But the real danger would be a situation in which the factors heightening tension radiated from Europe. It would be much more preferable for us to have a calming effect on a world burdened by so many peace-threatening pressures.

Although the present stability in Europe could be maintained at a considerably lower level of armament than at present, the arms race continues to accelerate. Claiming to be striving for balance, one side is introducing weapons which the other views as destabilizing and hence requiring counter-armament. These new weapons already constitute a threat to countries outside the military alliances. Therefore, every effort to promote negotiations that could hinder this development and steer a course towards disarmament has Finland's unreserved support.

For as long as détente has been striven for, it has encountered opposition as well. To those who see international politics as a kind of zero-total game, in which one side can only benefit at the other's expense, every single step towards détente looks like a policy of surrender. It is in this spirit that a struggle has been and is being waged, especially within the Western European camp.

Finland, which is sufficiently small and suitably remote, has been wielded as a cudgel in this propaganda war, which appears only to have heated up in recent times.

The word "Finlandization" has become rooted in international political terminology. It is meant to represent Finland as a cautionary example of a country that has fared badly by cultivating friendly relations with the Soviet Union.

It is obvious that those who use that word possess no knowledge of our country's history nor present-day circumstances; none, at least, worth mentioning.

Finland's position and policies can be understood only if one recalls the state in which the country found itself during the final stages of the Second World War. Her people demonstrated a strong enough desire and an adequate ability to live an independent life. She pulled through thanks to the statesmanship displayed by presidents Paasikivi and Kekkonen in the post-war period. This was based on a correct assessment of our national interests and geopolitical position. The decisive factor was the adoption of a new policy in relation to the Soviet Union. Only by taking our neighbour's vital security interests into consideration could Finland safeguard her own basic interests, sovereignty and independence.

Finland has exercised restraint in her stances on international issues; excessively so in the view of many. But if the intention is to set us up as a negative example to others, we have nothing to be ashamed of nor to apologize for. The positions that we have adopted in relation to the Soviet Union's policies, for example, must be examined in the context of our generally restrained line in international questions.

Relations between Finland and the Soviet Union were characterized by mistrust right up to the 1940s, but today they are founded on mutual respect. Since both countries acknowledge each other's fundamental interests, which are defined in the 1948 Treaty of Friendship, Co-operation and Mutual Assistance, the prerequisites for creating a policy of genuine friendship between neighbours have been at hand.

Those who talk of Finlandization imply that we have lost something of our sovereignty and independence as a consequence of our policy of friendship towards the Soviet Union. But the facts indicate that the opposite is the case: Finland has been able to develop on the basis of her own social system and has gained recognition as a fully-fledged member of the international community. Surely the best proof that our policy suits our interests is the fact that it enjoys broad, indeed, virtually unanimous support among our citizens.

There is a tendency in the Western press to

measure independence in decibels: the louder a country criticizes its neighbour's conditions and policies, the more independent it is. Those who gauge independence in this way, do not assess our actions in the light of expediency, but rather of conspicuousness. We, on the other hand, are interested in the final result: how best to promote our national interests and the most appropriate way to contribute to international development.

We believe that reinforcing peace and promoting disarmament are in the interests of both the East and the West. We have no desire to speak badly of others, and where our Eastern neighbour is concerned, we know that it wants peace, that it wants a general limitation of armament, and that an accelerating and increasingly expensive arms race is not in its interests.

However selfishly she may pursue her own interests, Finland can play a role in safeguarding peace in Europe. Were she to deviate from her policy of neutrality and harmonious neighbourly relations and thus upset the prevailing stable situation in Northern Europe, it would not be in the interests of her neighbours in either East or West.

Today's Finnish society is characterized by a greater degree of consensus and a more developed capacity for co-operation than ever before in our history. Our democratic system enjoys the broad approval and support of our citizens. President

Kekkonen devoted his entire career as a states-
man to strengthening national unity by encouraging the political centre and left to co-operate on
a long-term basis. The Finnish people is to all
intents and purposes unanimous in its support of
our foreign policy, which is called the Paasikivi-
Kekkonen Line.

There have been times in our history when our
decision makers have felt themselves prevented by
public opinion from making the kind of con-
cessions in foreign relations that they otherwise
considered advisable. At times, such situations
can culminate awkwardly in crises. A government
must conduct its policy in a manner that gains the
citizens's approval. If it does not, it must resign.

But in a crisis, a government must adopt
solutions that it seriously believes to be the wisest
ones from the viewpoints of both the state and its
citizens.

One of the basic goals of Finnish foreign policy
has been to ensure that the constructive atmosphere in Northern Europe is further strengthened. A nuclear-weapons-free status is an essential sub-factor in this. We believe that all states
consider it to be in their own interests to preserve
the prevailing stable situation in this region. That
will also remain one of the permanent goals of
Finnish foreign policy.

The negative effects of an incessant arms race

23

are making themselves particularly clearly felt in Europe, which is now the most heavily armed continent on earth. It is difficult to imagine that the security of our continent can be improved by continually introducing new and more destructive weapon systems. Security can only be built on a basis of systematic arms control and reduction of armament levels, especially where nuclear weapons are concerned.

Finland is part of Europe. Political and military developments in our continent affect our security as well. That is why we have on several occasions expressed our concern over the possibility that the Geneva talks on intermediate-range nuclear missile systems will break down. The same concern applies to negotiations between the Soviet Union and the United States concerning strategic weapons. Failure could easily lead to an acceleration of the arms race. It is now justified to urge the partners to show willingness to negotiate: no opportunity should be left unused in efforts to reach agreement.

The Nordic nuclear-weapons-free zone can not be an alternative to general control of armament or broadly-based decisions on disarmament. However, such a zone would, to a limited extent, enhance the security of this region. It should also be borne in mind that the Nordic countries are de facto already a nuclear-weapons-free zone in

24

peacetime. When he presented his idea, President Kekkonen said that its implementation would correspond to everybody's interests, but would be directed against nobody. It is in that way that the zone would enhance security.

We have not defined our stance on this question in detail. Nor were we overjoyed when some Norwegians and Swedes presented rather far-reaching conclusions concerning the character of the zone.

The Soviet Union has mainly announced its stances on the ideas presented by the Norwegians and the Swedes. In fact, the Soviet Union has not proposed anything; it has merely reacted.

Although the scheme primarily concerns the Nordic countries, it is, nevertheless, obvious that it cannot be implemented without the involvement of the nuclear powers. A nuclear-weapons-free Nordic region can not be brought into being in isolation from everything else. It must be part of a broader totality. The question still being pondered is whether the Nordic countries want to develop the idea into part of a more comprehensive plan.

The security of Europe, like that of all other nations, is nowadays no longer just a military matter. Endeavours to improve European security should also include a patient and determined effort to accomplish better co-operation and contacts between people, transcending the boundary lines that divide our continent. In this endeavour, the Helsinki Final Act remains a central instrument that has demonstrated its value. The results achieved to date, although in many important respects they fail to meet our expectations, have proved valuable. At the same time, we are aware that there is a constant need for progress in all sub-areas of the CSCE process, security issues and the spheres of economic co-operation and humanitarian questions, if the process is to bring real benefits to our peoples.

Finland is fortunate to be located in a part of Europe from which few reports of dramatic political changes have generally gone out to the world. The Nordic societies are stable and interaction between them constant and free of problems.

But their history does contain many dramatic events and disappointments. The period 1939—45 taught the small peoples of Northern Europe many important facts. Those experiences were to have a central influence on the security-policy solutions devised by each Nordic country after the Second World War. Since then, the region has been characterized by uninterrupted stability. Every one of the Nordic countries pursues a policy aimed at maintaining this stable situation and tries wherever possible to take the other countries into consideration in important decisions concerning the security-policy sphere.

For the Finns, the Second World War ended to all intents and purposes in autumn 1944. However, we still had to expel German forces from the northern part of our country and face up to the task of building up a new kind of relationship with our large Eastern neighbour.

We in Finland have thus far examined the war in Lapland mainly from the perspective of our fulfilling the terms of the Armistice Agreement with the Soviet Union, stressing the fact that we demonstrated our ability to implement one difficult part of the agreement.

However, the fighting in Lapland also has another aspect: it was a war in which Finland participated alongside the Allies in wearing down Nazi Germany's war machine.

It was certainly not easy for everybody to launch merciless warfare towards the north. The fighting was done by the same army that had been at war against Soviet forces for over three years. But the Germans made it somewhat easier for many Finnish soldiers by attacking the Finns in the south, on the island of Suursaari.

It is possible that the Germans would have withdrawn from Lapland more easily if the Finns had not begun expelling them from there. By advancing determinedly the Finns tied down German forces and hindered their use on other fronts. Finnish pressure forced the Germans to destroy their supplies and abandon their equipment.

The Soviet troops who had been fighting on the Finnish front were freed for deployment elsewhere. The Finnish northward advance also made some other operations that the Soviet Union had planned against the Germans unnecessary, and thus even more troops were available for service in other sectors.

The Germans had had plans to occupy southern Finland. They sought an opposition movement amenable to them, but in vain. Fortunately for us, Soviet forces quickly drove the Germans out of the area on the southern shore of the Gulf of Finland, and thus the threat to us from that quarter was eliminated.

The last German forces were driven across the border near Kilpisjärvi on 27 April, 1945.

3. A Policy of Good Neighbourly Relations

The President's most central task is to conduct Finland's relations with foreign states, determine the outlines of her foreign policy and participate in its implementation.

I was once asked by a journalist to define the contents of Finnish foreign policy in only three words. I answered: "good neighbourly relations." Astonished, he asked: "Is that enough for you?"

If Finland's relations with her closest neighbours, the Soviet Union and the other Nordic countries, are not in order, it will be futile to try to construct a credible role in any broader international context.

Foreign policy is often understood in a narrower sense to mean our bilateral relations, above all those with neighbouring countries.

In a broader sense, however, it could also be called "international policy". There is unlikely to be any change in procedural methods as regards the way in which Finland participates in international politics, above all at the United Nations and in other fora. Indeed, Finland has been quite active in multilateral relations.

It was as part of the Russian Empire that Finland developed and matured into an independent state. That would certainly not have been the case under Swedish rule and it prompts interesting questions. The answers will, naturally, remain in the sphere of guesswork, but it would be interesting to know what Finland would look like today. Would our fate have been the same as Ireland's?

Finland's separate development began when Napoleon and Czar Alexander divided Europe between them at Tilsit. Russia was given Finland, which for long thereafter remained as though torn loose from something. In the political sense, the country belonged to Russia, but for a long period retained Swedish laws and currency. In other respects, however, the process of integration with Swedish society had been halted and the result of this was that Finland developed her own social institutions, with the exception of a foreign affairs administration. Indeed, there was development even in that sphere, because Finland conducted her foreign trade independently and maintained her own consular service.

Her relationship with Russia was such that it implied, to a varying degree, a need to take or to refrain from taking stances on external matters. J.V. Snellman's advocacy of caution and restraint during the Polish Revolt in 1863 is a good example. And during the First World War, Finland, although part of the Russian Empire, was not a belligerent. I recall my father telling about the fate of a sailing ship on which he was a carpenter at the time. It was boarded by a landing party from a German submarine, which would have allowed it to proceed on its way as a "Russian-Finnish", i.e. neutral vessel, had it not been carrying a cargo of saltpeter, one of the ingredients of gunpowder, bound for England. I have often reflected on how that could have been possible. One can not really say that Finland was truly neutral, but although Russian troops were stationed in the country, she was not at war, either.

Viewed from today's perspective, Russia was indeed oppressing Finland. That is how it looked then, and that is undoubtedly how it was. But on the other hand, the situation was not always quite so simple. To take one example, the government in St. Petersburg tried to conscript Finland's youth into the Czarist army, but when the Finns resisted this, the Czarist authorities backed down. It can, of course, be argued that Finland participated economically in Russia's war effort, and a huge sum in receivables had accumulated by the time of the Russian Revolution.

In the economic sense, Finland became deeply integrated with Western Europe during the period of Russian rule. This was due to the fact that our industry was primarily based on wood processing and the natural markets for its products were in Western Europe. By contrast, our exports of metal products mainly went to Russia, and in this respect independence and the ensuing upheaval in our trade relations proved awkward.

The basic goal of our foreign policy during the entire post-war period has been to ensure peace and safeguard the conditions essential for the growth of the immaterial and material welfare of our nation.

Paasikivi's view of the world was a very pessimistic one. He saw international politics as a "great power concert", in which the role accorded small nations is not an enviable one. On the other hand, a desire for independence and acknowledgement of the right and obligation of every nation to defend itself were inseparable parts of his thinking. It was at his explicit wish that this principle was given eloquent expression in the first article of the Treaty of Friendship, Cooperation and Mutual Assistance. It constitutes a stand on the security problem of small nations in a situation in which disarmament is not progressing and no general system has been created for the peaceful settlement of conflicts.

Finland's security and solid international position have been built up since the Second World War, primarily through a skillful foreign policy, and the significance of this has only been enhanced by the frantic development of the superpowers' weapons technology.

The foundation for Finland's present foreign policy was created in the years immediately after the war. The fact that the cold winds that had already begun to blow in international politics did not prevent the Paris Peace Treaty from being concluded (in 1947) was extremely important to us. This treaty signified the normalization of our relations with all our war-time enemies and thus the stabilization of our international position. It was also in this period in the second half of the 1940s that the basic contents and broad lines of our foreign policy coalesced. One of the cardinal points here was the concept that foreign policy takes precedence over everything else in our national politics. Of foremost importance are our relations with the Soviet Union. A relationship of trust with our Eastern neighbour created the conditions necessary for us to develop good and friendly relations with all countries. The same basic conception is still part of our foreign policy approach, which is today called the Paasikivi-Kekkonen Line. Finland will consistently continue to follow this line during my term as president.

It is useful for two neighbouring countries living on amicable terms to build their mutual relations on a sufficiently long-term basis. This type of planning creates the security and dependability on which all co-operation must be practised and developed. In this respect the past few decades have shown what factors in relations between our two nations form a healthy and enduring foundation on which to build plans. Of central importance is the Treaty of Friendship, Co-operation and Mutual Assistance, on the basis of which we have over the years created a network of relations unparalled by few others. Also extremely important are the trust-based and

35

sincere personal relations which have traditionally existed between our countries' leaders.

Whether one speaks of an idealistic foreign
policy or of a realistic one, the use of the adjective,
whichever it is, is justified in one and the same
way if one imagines a line between two extremes,
with every nation having to find its proper place
on that line. It is hardly conceivable that any state
could pursue a purely idealistic or purely realistic
policy, although, of course, one always tries to use
those terms to label countries' foreign policies.
The superpowers, in particular, seemingly have to
pursue policies that at times appear very selfish.

Finland's policy of neutrality is based first and
foremost on a desire to maintain good relations
with our neighbouring countries and retain their
trust. Alongside this, we want to have friendly
relations with all of the world's nations.

Our impact on world affairs is understandably
limited. However, we remain determined to make
whatever contribution we can to restraining
international conflicts and promoting peaceful
solutions.

4. Finland and the Soviet Union

It would be well to remember what J.K. Paasikivi said in a farewell interview in the Swedish daily *Dagens Nyheter* in summer 1955 (he retired in 1956): "The most important thing for Finland is and will always be the preservation of good relations with Russia. Geography and history dictate that so it must be."

Paasikivi said this at a time when the Second World War was fresh in people's minds and the Cold War still in progress. Although a considerable change for the better has taken place in the international situation, the basic substance of Paasikivi's message retains its applicability. He had learnt his history and he knew that certain realities of international politics do not change.

The illusion that one can take a speculator's approach to the management of international trends is dangerous and deceptive.

I believe that there are — or at least have been — many people in Finland holding the firm conviction that the Soviet Union constitutes a great threat to us, and I also believe that there are many people abroad who consider this the most natural of things. We have had two wars with the Soviet Union. The first was the Winter War, which lasted over three months in 1939—40, and then there was another, known in Finnish history as the Continuation War, lasting over three years from 1941 to 1944. Since these wars, our relations have developed very well. I am not aware of a single instance in which the Soviet Union has behaved differently to what she has said she would or done anything other than what had been agreed upon. On the contrary, we have every reason to believe that our relations have been finally settled. They are good.

The basis on which Fenno-Soviet relations have developed has been the 1948 Treaty of Friendship, Co-operation and Mutual Assistance, which created the conditions necessary for mutual trust. In this treaty Finland promises to use all available forces to repel any armed attack on herself or on the Soviet Union through Finnish territory. As an independent state, she would do that in any case. If need be, the Treaty further states, the Soviet Union will provide us with assistance, the nature of which would be agreed upon between us. Should a threat of an attack be perceived, Finland and the Soviet Union will hold consultations with each other.

The preamble to the Treaty acknowledges "Finland's desire to remain outside the conflicting interest of the Great Powers". President Paasikivi had particularly wanted such a provision to be included and had authorized Urho Kekkonen to negotiate the matter as his personal representative. This part of the Treaty was later to be of central importance when Urho Kekkonen, having succeeded Paasikivi, began to develop Finland's policy of neutrality and to give it its present active, peace-oriented content.

The Treaty is a totality in which every part is important. Nothing has happened to give us any reason to put new interpretations on it.

The articles in the Treaty that deal with co-operation have been supplemented by numerous documents concerning a variety of fields. The most important of these in the economic sphere are a 1971 treaty providing for the development of economic, teachnical and industrial co-operation and a long-range programme concerning co-operation in this field, which was signed during President Kekkonen's state visit to the Soviet Union in 1977.

Three and a half decades represent more than half the period since Finland became independent. These years have been very positive; they have brought us peace and security as well as fruitful interaction with our neighbours and other peoples. That has been the prerequisite for the growth of our national prosperity.

We have every reason to be very satisfied with the results that we have experienced in applying the Treaty to changing international political and economic circumstances in the course of those decades. This indicates the far-sightedness of those Finns and Soviets who gave the Treaty its contents in 1948, contents that are still valid today.

Our mutual relations have developed on a basis of trust and independently of fluctuations in the international situation. This fact is of quite

41

particular importance now that tension in the world, and here in Europe too, has been increasing at an alarming rate.

The Treaty has provided the firm foundation on which our determined work has enabled us to build up a multifaceted network of co-operation covering almost all spheres of life. Today, we can be satisfied with the fruit that this tree of co-operation continues to yield.

The positive effects of good neighbourly relations between our countries have more than merely a bilateral dimension. The Treaty has significantly contributed to the stable security situation in Northern Europe. Finland and the Soviet Union are making their own active contributions to efforts on behalf of détente and disarmament, international peace and co-operation.

Meetings between Finnish and Soviet leaders and the amicable and cordially open talks conducted on these occasions have contributed significantly to the development of our mutual relations in a manner benefiting both countries and peoples. In recent years the importance of these meetings has constantly grown.

Economic co-operation has traditionally had a pre-eminent role in Fenno-Soviet relations. The Soviet Union has long been our most significant trading partner. It is now our most important source of imports and largest export market. Finland, too, has a well-established position as one of the Soviet Union's leading Western trade associates. In this connection I would like to emphasize the instrumental role played by President Urho Kekkonen also in the successful development of our nations' economic relations.

In recent years we have noted with great pleasure the intense growth that has taken place in our commercial dealings with the Soviet Union. Increasing trade is practical proof of the long-term nature of economic co-operation between our two countries. It also demonstrates that our framework of bilateral agreements and the clearing system which is part of it have provided excellent conditions for developing trade.

The main outlines of future economic relations between Finland and the Soviet Union are set down in a long-range programme signed in 1977. This programme was updated and extended to the end of 1995 in a special protocol which was signed at the highest level in Moscow in 1980. I hope that we shall also be able to continue developing our nations' economic co-operation on the established basis of agreements, which have proved beneficial to both parties.

In the Kostamus project, the construction of a major industrial complex and a fair-sized city around a huge deposit of iron ore in the north-eastern part of the Soviet Union, we see an outstanding example of the results that good neighbourly relations based on trust between our countries can bring.

As great as the impact of Kostamus has been on trade between our countries, it is by no means limited to trade. It has also stimulated the economy of Eastern and North-Eastern Finland and provided work for thousands. Joint projects of this kind have for years been accounting for 10—15 per cent of our exports to the Soviet Union. Construction has thus become an integral part of our trade; in addition to huge complexes near the border, we have built hotels, power stations and smaller industrial plants. We are currently supplying compressor stations and helping to build entire residential communities along the gas pipeline from the Soviet Union to Western Europe.

Once the major projects now in progress have been completed, this kind of co-operation will presumably continue in our border regions, thanks to the experience that we have gained and our geographical advantage. Preliminary discussions have already been held concerning several new sizable projects. In time, the traditional pattern of large-scale construction will be complemented by new forms of export. A recent example is provided by various types of structures and industrial plants to be assembled by the client upon delivery in the Soviet Union. The contracts may include start-up supervision. Deals of this kind give hundreds of Finnish companies a new door to trade between our two countries, enabling them, to build plants in remote regions of the Soviet Union on a turnkey basis.

As I see it, we enjoy all the preconditions for furthering our economic relations. The current limiting factor on Finnish exports, our payments surplus, is a temporary phenomenon which we shall balance out through mutual effort. In fact, the groundwork has already been laid, and the solution soon to emerge is based on Finnish needs and interests. The Soviet Union has not asked for credit but we have ourselves suggested additional time to enable us to balance our trade over a longer period and so safeguard the continuity of our traditional exports.

We Finns must draw similar conclusions also with regard to our imports. In co-operation with the Soviet Union, we have built a top-quality steel mill in Finland, along with two nuclear power stations boasting capacity utilization rates among the highest in the world. We must now address ourselves to the task of finding opportunities to implement other Soviet projects in Finland.

Here our long term co-operation programme provides plenty of stimuli, and I believe that some new projects will be launched in the near future. Alongside large projects, we are turning our attention to smaller-scale schemes in sectors in which the Soviet Union can offer particularly advanced technology.

Joint Fenno-Soviet projects in third countries are also gradually beginning to bear fruit in the form

45

of concrete tenders that can be expected to lead to solid contracts.

Our shared, constant aim is to diversify Finnish imports from the Soviet Union. For Finland this is a major concern, because trade represents such a large segment of our national economy that even minor fluctuations in the world-market prices of some of our main imports can have major repercussions on us. I hope, therefore, that both Finnish companies and the authorities, in particular the Fenno-Soviet Joint Trade Commission, will bear these aspects in mind at all times.

The picture of Fenno-Soviet economic relations is not complete without our co-operation in the sphere of production, which boosts the grand transactions total and promotes imports and exports on both sides.

Opportunities for co-operation abound, in fields ranging from the exchange of raw materials to subcontracting and joint production and marketing. Each item may constitute and often has constituted an entire industrial project, of which several examples are nearing completion. These include the manufacture of locomotives and ship-building-related projects. Our latest achievement is co-operation in electronic communications technology, in respect of which a protocol is now being drafted.

A further point that I should like to make in this connection is that the Kostamus project has also promoted our scientific and technical co-operation.

The agreements that we have concluded include one covering the development of testing methods for use in building. Kostamus has also provided a splendid opportunity for co-operation between community planning experts in both countries. The construction of the city is to be the subject of a planned report, which will certainly prove useful in future joint projects.

Kostamus has become a new bond between our countries. Here numerous builders from Finland and Soviet Karelia have become friends both at and outside work. We hope that in due time Kostamus will play a prominent role in trade conducted under special arrangements for our frontier regions. These arrangements have long stimulated trade between Finland and Soviet Karelia.

It is probably because Kostamus is so symbolic of long-term economic co-operation between Finland and the Soviet Union that it has attracted so much attention not only in those countries, but elsewhere as well.

Compared with other Western countries, Finland enjoys a special position in Soviet trade in the respect that the Soviet Union agrees to have payments transacted through a clearing account. This regular trade is to our advantage in many respects, because it is free and based on long-term agreements. It has very often succeeded in offsetting cyclical fluctuations originating in the

West and the structure of this trade has been quite advantageous from our point of view.

Finland's position in the world of today is better than it might sometimes appear to us, living here in the midst of our own problems. It should make us realize the importance of the consistent policy of neutrality that we pursue.

That policy is founded on good relations with the Soviet Union. That we pursue our own interests — sometimes, perhaps, even selfishly — does not make us bad neighbours; rather, the opposite is the case. We are not involved in any adventurous policies, but represent a permanent and predictable line in the corner of the world that is our home.

In the last few years, we have been able to diverge, to our advantage, from the general economic development in the Western industrial countries. That has been possible because the prices of our export products have developed favourably and also because we have been able to pay our growing bill for oil imports from the Soviet Union with exports. The domestic costs level has been kept in check and thus our industry's price competitiveness has improved.

In international politics we are going through a difficult period, which easily creates a sense of insecurity in relation to the position and intentions of different states. Finland's position in this situation is, however, beyond any speculation or conjecture. We shall continue steadfastly to follow the Paasikivi-Kekkonen Line.

The stability of our international position has been decisively enhanced by the fact that for over three and a half decades our relations with our superpower neighbour, the Soviet Union, have been founded on a basic agreement whose contents have remained unaltered. That is why we considered it desirable to extend the Treaty of Friendship, Co-operation and Mutual Assistance in its present form before the expiry date. For its part, the leadership of the Soviet Union has expressed its willingness in this respect. Since it happened also in 1955 and 1970, extending the Treaty well ahead of time has become a good tradition.

The signing of a protocol extending the validity of the Treaty for 20 years is concrete proof of the continuity and unchanged nature of our relations based on mutual trust, and enables us to contemplate our relations well into the future as well. I personally consider it very important that this extension of the document so fundamental to our relations took place during my first state visit to the Soviet Union. It gave the visit an important political dimension.

Thanks to the far-sightedness of those who gave the Treaty its form, Finland and the Soviet Union enjoy exemplary neighbourly relations which are not affected by fluctuations in the international climate or different political trends. Experience has shown that these relations are compatible with the basic interests of both countries and peoples in every respect.

5. Between the Nordic Countries

The affinity between the peoples of the Nordic region rests on a millenium of tradition, but it is only in the past three decades or so that our mutual co-operation has really intensified and expanded to virtually every sphere of life. Our Nordic identity has strengthened at the same time as we have been able to participate in broader European and international interaction as well.

Although Finland did not take part in the work of the Nordic Council until four years after that body had been established, there has never been any doubt that our nation belongs to the Nordic community and is willing to participate in co-operation within this framework.

We Finns shall also continue to support the development and expansion of this co-operation on an established basis.

The past 30 years have seen profound changes in the forms and contents of Nordic co-operation. However, there have been no changes in some of the basic premises on which the work of the Nordic Council is arranged, nor will there be any reason to alter them in the future, either.

Indeed, as Urho Kekkonen pointed out in a speech in January 1956, the Nordic Council was established to work for peace and humane progress.

When Finland became a member of the Nordic Council in 1956, one of the conditions stipulated by the Finnish Government was that the Council would continue to refrain from dealing with foreign-policy or security-policy questions. By contrast, these questions can be discussed by, for example, the Nordic foreign ministers. The different security-policy solutions adopted by the Nordic countries have not prevented these countries from often having similar views on international issues. This would appear to have manifested itself most clearly at the United Nations and in its sub-agencies.

We have been able to discuss our own important security-policy solutions openly and in a spirit of neighbourliness. Although our points of departure differ from each other, I have been able to note with satisfaction that the aim is to adapt our respective solutions to the ultimate goal: that of preserving a stable and peaceful situation in the Nordic region.

Every now and then, a very unpleasant situation arises at meetings of the Nordic Council, when security policy nevertheless becomes the subject of debate and largely Pharisiacal attitudes are displayed. Many of those who deplore speeches on the subject in question impatiently await the slightest provocation in order to be able to participate in the debate and expand it even further.

If members of parliament feel a need to discuss security policy, they have ample opportunities to do so in numerous fora outside the Nordic Council each year. I have not noticed any need for a new forum.

The Nordic character, Nordic affinity and Nordic co-operation are themes that are often taken up in festive speeches. A prestigious observer has noted, with some embarrassment, that occasional lapses into "tinsely phraseology" occur in the context of Nordic contacts, something that can be attributed to the somewhat ceremonious character of the Nordic peoples.

At its best, co-operation consists of everyday toil with all its joys and sorrows, and in my view the person who said that Nordic co-operation was more a cross-frontier extension of the participating countries' domestic policies than foreign policy came close to the truth. Anybody who has been involved in domestic politics knows how superfluous fancy phrases are in this sphere. Except, of course, in the run-up to elections.

The centuries during which no national frontier separated Finland and Sweden led in most respects to our two countries developing in similar manners. It was then that the foundation for our social development was laid and a bond, which still exists today, forged.

External circumstances and both nations' deliberate efforts to foster their unique national characters have led them to develop in their own directions. Nevertheless, our view of life and the foundation on which the life of our citizens is built are in the most essential respects shared by both. In devising our social systems we have followed the same basic principles in which the individual's right to and work for social equality have had a central position.

Nordic affinity and co-operation between our nations have led to natural and fruitful dealings in all spheres of today's society. Cultural exchanges between our nations are very broad and rewarding. No doubt Finnish immigration to Sweden has also played a significant role in this. In economic co-operation we have recorded achievements which no one could have imagined two decades ago. Our co-operation in the political field has likewise been thought-provoking, inspiring, and has had a great practical significance. We have every reason to assume that these contacts will continue to be of great importance to our peoples.

The Nordic countries have chosen different solutions in their security policies — Finland and Sweden clear, though not identical policies of neutrality. These solutions and our wide-ranging co-operation have made the Nordic region unique in today's troubled world. Our peoples have not wanted to isolate themselves from various international co-operative endeavors, but have, rather, been aware that they have an important role to play in achieving peace and détente in Europe and the whole world.

The Nordic countries' mutual relations have become better, but we must ask ourselves whether we could not do more to improve the situation in the region. Discussions between us are conducted in a positive atmosphere. In my view, there is a great need to work for an improvement in the situation in the world in general, especially where relations between the superpowers are concerned. The UN provides us with a forum for this. In most questions that have arisen there, the Nordic countries have adopted a united stance. And nowadays we meet each other more often than we used to — the prime ministers at least three times a year, and the foreign ministers and senior civil servants rather frequently as well. These meetings provide excellent opportunities for exchanges of views.

Viewed against the background of a broader international context, the situation in Northern Europe is stable and peaceful. That is all the more noteworthy when one considers that relations between the superpowers have been tensing at an alarming rate, concurrent with an increase in their interest in the northernmost part of Europe. It is obvious that it would not be in the interests of anybody, least of all the Nordic countries, if the situation were to be transformed into an unstable one. Regional co-operation schemes remain of central importance in efforts to reduce tension and enhance security.

A phenomenon like Nordic co-operation is extremely rare in today's world. Hardly anywhere else do sovereign states work so closely together and in so many spheres as do the Nordic countries.

For decades, Nordic co-operation has enabled us to develop our region and increase its prosperity. Differences concerning security policy, and in some respects economic policy as well, have not prevented our countries' stances on international questions from being similar in quite many cases.

In their security policies, Iceland, Norway and Denmark have opted for membership of a military alliance; Sweden and Finland have remained neutral. It goes without saying that each government takes its security-policy decisions — like other decisions — on its own. In so doing the Nordic countries have, however, always considered how their decisions will affect the situation of the other Nordic nations. Co-operation on the basis of these principles has gone well.

At times when international developments are giving rise to serious apprehension, it is important that the Nordic countries have such good and confidential relations that they can talk frankly with each other. I am convinced that no Nordic nation consciously wishes to heighten tension in our continent. From Finland's point of view, the military limitations imposed by the Nordic countries are important, and we naturally hope that nothing will happen to cause any substantial change in this situation.

The tragic events that the world has witnessed in recent times and the human suffering caused by them have deeply shocked us Finns. At the same time we have been seriously troubled by the spectacle of the UN being thrust aside — even in a humiliating manner — from its central task, peacekeeping and mediation with the aim of creating peace. We believe that means should be sought to enable the world organization's authority to be re-established in this respect. Here, the Nordic countries are in a position to produce initiatives in this important matter and to be of service to other countries.

6. Nordic Security

The Nordic region is an essential part of the European system of security and equilibrium. Its strategic and military importance has grown in the course of the years. However, it must be emphasized that the stable security-policy configuration that has prevailed in the region since the Second World War continues, in the view of the Finnish Government, to correspond to the interests of all the Nordic countries and is also in harmony with the interests of all other states to which, in one way or another, developments in the region are relevant.

Like all other states, Finland has a legitimate right to ensure her own security and towards this end she has presented initiatives on questions concerning the security of the Nordic region. The intention has been to reinforce the existing stable security-policy situation and care has been taken to allow for developments in the fields of military policies and arms technology.

Security policy has been the subject of lively debate in all of the Nordic countries in recent times, with concern for the future the dominant theme throughout. Although the nature of the debate in each individual country is, naturally, an internal matter for that country, the Finnish Government has kept a close eye on its course. It is our wish that the debate will eventually contribute to promoting efforts to establish a nuclear-weapons-free zone in the Nordic region. Although views on the various political, military and regional parameters relating to the zone have not yet led to compatible conclusions, the fact that safeguarding the existing nuclear-weapons-free status of the region has become the subject of serious political deliberation must be considered a positive step forward.

There is every justification for stating that Nordic co-operation has developed favourably in the difficult years of the past as well. There are no major problems between the Nordic countries, and especially no insoluble ones. To those who would like to see something dramatic and exciting in Nordic co-operation, the present situation may, of course, appear problematic, but most of us see Nordic co-operation as an extension of our countries' domestic policies.

With the international situation giving rise to such grave concern, it is particularly important that relations between the Nordic countries be so good and characterized by trust that these countries can discuss things frankly. I am convinced that none of them consciously wants to increase tension in this part of the world. The military limits voluntarily observed by the Nordic countries are valuable from Finland's point of view, and we naturally hope that nothing will happen to cause a significant alteration in this situation.

The situation in Northern Europe has, fortunately, not altered, but remained stable. However, we are aware that our region is not an island separated from the rest of the world, but an area easily affected by changes in the international situation over which we have no control. The Nordic countries have striven determinedly to achieve and maintain peaceful and stable conditions in general, especially in our own part of the world. Both Sweden and Finland have given their uncompromising support to efforts to promote détente. In today's situation, this work is more important than it has ever been.

Norway has herself imposed clear restraints on her security policy, especially in relation to nuclear weapons and military bases. It is primarily a matter for the Norwegians themselves to interpret the situation in this respect. And it is the country's own business if it keeps within the framework of the policy that it has defined, but it is also understandable that others hold views on the matter. When, for example, an American news report claims that Norway has changed her policy and the Soviets rapidly pick up the issue, claim the same and criticize Norway, it is natural that everything connected with the matter interests Finland. To put it in a nutshell: Finland wants to believe that Norway has not altered her security policy and does not want to alter it over the long term, either. We Nordic countries must demonstrate trust in and solidarity with each other in such questions. However, we are aware that our room for manoeuvre in this sphere is very limited.

Finland's initiatives to increase security in the northern part of Europe are still on the table. We have a continuing interest in agreements of greater scope than at present, which would ensure that the border between Finland and Norway will remain a peaceful border even in any future international crisis situation. The idea of a Nordic nuclear-free zone has gained a significant number of new supporters in the other Nordic countries since 1979.

There has been much talk of a border pacification treaty between Finland and Norway, but for my own part I have tried to avoid the use of the word "treaty". When it is said that there is no need for a treaty, one could understand that a formal agreement of this kind is superfluous. At the same time, we have repeatedly pointed out that our interests run parallel to each other and that what is involved is how we could increase the degree of reciprocity in our statements and assurances to the effect that we want to bolster peace in our region and ensure that our borders remain peaceful in the future as well. Thus several possibilities are available, provided we avoid striving for formal treaties, which would be difficult to formulate and implement.

The good neighbourly relations that exist between Finland and the Soviet Union have remained unaltered. We have made it clear that we want friendship with the Soviet Union. The Soviets are somewhat conservative; they want to preserve the present situation. They do not want to change it. If they did, things would look different from what they are. I have often asked myself whether all the mistrust that smoulders in the Nordic region is necessary. Shouldn't we be able to lessen tension and increase the degree of trust between our countries?

In an uneasy world, the situation looks relatively good. It must, however, be borne in mind that our global interdependence, for example in the sphere of technological development, is constantly growing. The big question is to what extent individual states can disengage themselves from the general development in a way that permits them to create a greater than average degree of security for their citizens and their immediate environment.

We have no exceptionally major problems. By contrast, our starting point is good in that we enjoy good relations with our neighbours. It would, of course, be preferable if our neighbours were to have better relations with each other than is sometimes the case. But we have not found ourselves in the awkward situation of an intermediary.

We have clear international agreements and the Treaty of Friendship, Co-operation and Mutual Assistance with the Soviet Union. When that beneficial document was concluded, it clarified our security-policy situation.

Finland needs capable defence forces. The main question is what degree of choice we actually have. As far as the treaties to which we are party are concerned, the Treaty of Friendship, Co-operation and Mutual Assistance requires Finland to defend her territory by all means at her disposal. And that is how it should be. The 1947 Paris Peace Treaty and the Armistice Agreement that preceded it had a somewhat different orientation in that they contained limitations on the quality and capacity of our defensive capability.

Technical development of weapons is a major problem facing the defence forces of all countries. The level of performance rises, but so do costs. An army equipped with modern weapons is expensive.

We should understand that although our defence forces are being developed, at no time in the foreseeable future will their capability be decisively different from what it is at the moment.

A positive endeavour shared by all of us in the Nordic countries is to contribute to promoting détente in the world and to play our respective roles in maintaining and boosting stability in our own corner of the globe. That is a good attitude when one bears the possibility of future periods of uncertainty in mind.

Such situations naturally include those in which relations of the great powers are deteriorating or testing. And especially one in which the danger of a major war is imminent. The Nordic countries are awkwardly located if one thinks of conflicts associated with the latter possibility. After all, the Soviet Union has a large and important naval base in the immediate vicinity of the Nordic region, and a considerable portion of the Soviet missile forces is under the control of the navy. In any confrontation that might arise, Norway's military importance would be strongly accentuated. We should strive by every means possible to lessen possibilities of such a conflict developing.

Although Europe has been spared war since 1945, it still has the greatest concentration of armaments in the world. That makes it very important from Finland's point of view to safeguard the development of détente and promote disarmament. Such efforts are part of Finland's security.

It can be pointed out, as a general observation,

that the strategic importance of the northern parts of our continent has increased in the course of the past decade. However, there is nothing in view that would prompt the assumption that the military focal point in Europe has shifted northwards or that the immediate threat of war in our region has grown.

In the light of today's developments in weapons technology, our position between East and West is no longer as remote as it used to be. The core question in our position and in our security policy as a whole is that of retaining the Soviet Union's confidence that our actions are aimed at fulfilling the obligations of the Treaty of Friendship, Co-operation and Mutual Assistance and that we are capable of doing so.

The goal of our security policy is to preserve our independence as a state, remain uninvolved in conflicts and safeguard our citizens' means of livelihood. In order to achieve this, our state authorities have to perform a demanding task not only in their everyday functions, but also in contingency planning for exceptional conditions.

Foreign relations have clear pride of place in our security policy. The instruments which they provide must be constantly used in efforts to promote détente and maintain peace, especially here in our own continent.

By international standards, the situation in the Nordic region has been stable and peaceful, largely due to the fact that in practice it has been a nuclear-weapons-free zone.

However, the development of nuclear weapons and changing strategic doctrines relating to their use have projected their effects into our region as well.

It appears that there are more nuclear weapons in our immediate vicinity than we had calculated, and the threshold to their use can be much lower than we had thought.

But none of these changes has lessened the current relevance of the proposals made by President Kekkonen in 1963 and 1978. On the contrary, efforts to lessen tension and ward off the threat of nuclear war are more important than ever.

As I see it, the importance and current relevance of this matter have been understood in all of the Nordic countries, but each country has assessed its opportunities for practical measures on the basis of its own security-policy premises.

A Soviet offer to negotiate with the Nordic countries on measures concerning Soviet territory has added new perspectives in the ongoing discussion of a Nordic nuclear-weapons-free zone. There must be a businesslike and comprehensive study of opportunities and problems relating to the contribution that the great powers can make in this sphere, and which will be indispensable if progress is to be made.

The Nordic countries must continue to conduct

an open-minded exchange of views on this question, as was agreed at a meeting of foreign ministers in Copenhagen in September 1981.

Finland has long taken the view that it would be in the interests of all concerned to confirm the prevailing de facto situation and establish a nuclear-weapons-free zone. This idea has been gaining growing support in the other Nordic countries as well, although opinions remain substantially different in relation to what practical measures should be taken. Recent times have seen concrete indications of the importance accorded this question in all of the Nordic countries. Finland considers it an important achievement that the Nordic foreign ministers have been exchanging views on the issue since September 1981. Its importance is also highlighted by the fact that the Danish, Finnish and Swedish prime ministers as well as the Norwegian foreign minister all included a statement on the matter in their speeches at the second UN special session on disarmament. In this I see a small, but clearly positive step forward. There is every reason to persevere with efforts to safeguard the nuclear-weapons-free status of the Nordic region.

We in Finland have been quite cautious in relation to new initiatives, but we do have our own interests to watch. If we were to go beyond those bounds, the result might be more harm than benefit.

It is, for example, conceivable that the Nordic countries could simply declare themselves a nuclear-weapons-free zone, without the involvement of the nuclear powers. But if they want those powers to play a positive role in the creation of such a zone, e.g. by committing themselves to measures on their own territories or in their territorial waters, achieving a solution becomes a considerably more complicated process.

It is essential to note that relations between the superpowers are the most important factor of all. Compared with the broad range of negotiations that are conducted between the United States and the Soviet Union, regional arrangements like a Nordic nuclear-weapons-free zone are, after all, of marginal importance when what is involved is limiting nuclear weaponry and increasing mutual trust. However, this does not exclude regional agreements contributing to the achievement of those goals.

The stable situation with regard to security policy in the Nordic region is based on unilateral decisions by each individual country, and in the case of the Nordic NATO members applies to peacetime. Thus it has always contained a certain instability factor, which in Finland, at least, has not been security enhancing. Therefore President Kekkonen proposed in 1963 that the prevailing situation be confirmed in mutual undertakings between the Nordic countries. He emphasized that such an arrangement would notably consolidate the position of all states in the Nordic region without detriment to the interests of any outside power.

In the course of the past nearly 20 years, none of the Nordic countries has seen any need to alter the prevailing situation. As I see it, that does not diminish the relevance of the Kekkonen plan in any way. On the contrary, it would be in the interests of all the peoples in the Nordic region to consolidate the situation, which has proved its desirability.

Indeed, it has been possible to note in recent times that interest in a Nordic nuclear-weapons-free zone is on the increase. The matter has been the subject of keen discussion in Norway and has to a large extent been reflected in discussion in Sweden as well.

We Finns have not put forward any new ideas nor initiatives, but the debate has been reflected in our country, too. One of the extreme alternatives proposed has been the creation, by proclamation, of a zone comprising Finland and Sweden. The "maxi-maxi" line proposed by former cabinet secretary Leifland of the Swedish foreign ministry would include not only the Nordic countries, but also the Baltic Sea and its ports.

As far as I can see, the debate has been shifting away from such "maxi-maxi" ideas, but I should like to emphasize that an idea propounded specifically in Sweden and Norway is one to the effect that the inclusion of the Nordic countries only is not enough, but that there must be greater symmetry in any arrangement achieved. If anything is to come of the matter, there will first have to be mutual understanding between the Nordic countries, and so far this has not been adequately in evidence. The question that will arise after that is how the matter will be viewed by those countries which possess nuclear weapons. And it is obvious that the scheme will amount to nothing unless the nuclear powers give it their support.

If one starts from the premise that the zone must be created anyway, one must naturally ask what is the use of an arrangement that has come about through proclamation alone. If only two countries were to be involved in the scheme, the outcome might be more harm than good where future developments are concerned.

The Finnish Government's aim has been to exclude the country and its immediate vicinity from international tension.

One of the reasons why the situation in the Nordic region has remained stable is the fact that it is a nuclear-weapons-free zone in practice. However, this is the result of unilateral positions which are valid, in the cases of Norway and Denmark, in peacetime only. Although a de facto nuclear-weapons-free status is a valuable thing in itself, it would be better to have it permanently confirmed and recognized by the nuclear powers.

With this in mind, President Urho Kekkonen proposed in 1963 that a nuclear-weapons-free zone be established in the Nordic region. He stated then that a treaty arrangement of this kind would indisputably exclude the Nordic countries from the sphere of speculations engendered by the development of nuclear strategies.

President Kekkonen's underlying idea has not lost its current applicability; indeed, it has gained even greater importance in recent times.

The development of arms technology and of possibilities to use it in Northern Europe have increased the danger of the region being dragged into nuclear conflicts. President Kekkonen drew the inevitable conclusions from this development and in 1978 decided to explicate the idea that he had put forward in 1963. The Nordic countries should work for an arms control treaty that would as completely as possible shield the region from the effects of nuclear weapons strategies in general and from new developments in this technology in particular.

The security needs of all countries in the region, as interpreted by those countries themselves, should be considered the starting point for the arrangements proposed.

Although there are different views in the Nordic countries with regard to practical measures to ward off the threat caused by nuclear weapons, broad unanimity on the importance of the region's nuclear-weapons-free status now exists. Numerous civic organizations have done valuable work to mould a positive public opinion on the matter.

Confirming the existing nuclear-weapons-free status of the region is primarily a matter for the Nordic countries themselves, but implementation of the decisions that will have to be taken presupposes the active support of the nuclear powers. Although the zone thus imposes its own preconditions, a matter that is also at issue is what the Nordic countries themselves can do in practice to meet those requirements.

For its part, the Soviet Union has promised to respect the proposed zone and to provide guarantees for it. It has also announced its willingness to consider certain substantial measures applying to its own territory in the vicinity of the area proposed for inclusion in the zone and conducive to consolidating the nuclear-weapons-free status of the region.

None of the efforts that have been made in the past 20 years to ensure, through treaty arrangements, that the region will remain free of nuclear weapons whatever the circumstances has yielded results. However, recent years have witnessed a profound change in the attitudes of the other Nordic countries to President Kekkonen's idea. In itself, the ongoing debate on the matter is conducive to bolstering trust and security.

President Kekkonen's vision of a nuclear-weapons-free Nordic region is firmly anchored in the totality of our security policy. We shall continue to work determinedly for its realization.

From Finland's point of view, Swedish neutrality has been a very important thing. Likewise the fact that when Norway and Denmark joined NATO, they imposed limitations on their membership in that nuclear weapons may not be brought onto their territories in peacetime nor military bases established there. We consider it very important that such a configuration has emerged and been preserved. We sometimes follow signs on the horizon with concern, hoping against hope that nothing will happen to alter or destroy this situation. After all, some aspects of the world change and others do not. One thing that does not change is geography. Realms are located where they are. But military technology sometimes changes very rapidly and engenders new situations, which then give rise to speculation about the extent to which they will alter or jeopardize the prevailing stability.

Cruise missiles became the subject of debate over ten years ago, when relatively little was known about them. Now we know more. They may have a military significance of their own, but viewed from the political perspective, and especially from that of disarmament, they reveal many negative characteristics.

They are difficult, if not impossible, to detect and verify, in addition to which it is hard to tell whether or not they are armed with nuclear warheads.

There are plans to build several thousand of these missiles. Most of them will apparently be deployed in the northernmost regions of the globe, either on board surface vessels or submarines or on aircraft operating from northern bases.

These missiles are creating instability in the Nordic region. They also raise the question of the inviolability of neutral states' air spaces. Statements of reassurance issued in this respect should be greeted with satisfaction. However, we are not the only ones who need to be reassured. We must be prepared to counter any violation of our territory or air space.

In 1978, President Kekkonen appealed to the nuclear powers to ban or limit cruise missiles. This appeal is more relevant today than ever before.

We have continued our efforts to create a nuclear-weapons-free zone in the Nordic region and at the same time sought understanding for this on the part of the nuclear powers. We need their commitment that nuclear weapons will not be used in the region nor their use threatened.

The creation of a nuclear-weapons-free zone would be a way of reducing fear, lessening tension and strengthening the security of the states in the zone, without detriment to the interests of any outside power.

Our appeals for efforts towards the establishment of a nuclear-weapons-free zone and prohibition of cruise missiles do not stem from fear that the likelihood of a nuclear war being unleashed in Europe has increased. On the contrary, recent developments seem to have weakened the credibility of theories that a limited nuclear war is possible. It is quite widely believed that the first use of nuclear weapons would inevitably lead to their widespread use, and thus threatening to use them has become a threat of mutual destruction.

7. A Peace-Oriented Policy of Neutrality

In accordance with the Paasikivi-Kekkonen Line, Finland has endeavoured to build up relations founded on mutual understanding and trust with all the states in the world. Pursuing an active, peace-oriented policy of neutrality, we desire to be able to contribute to strengthening international security, especially here in Europe. It is my view that détente must continue, growing international tension notwithstanding. Peacetime is the time to build peace.

Urho Kekkonen's point of departure was the same geographical and political realism which Snellman and Paasikivi represented at its purest. But whereas for Paasikivi the best peace work small nations could perform was to improve the intellectual and material life of their own peoples, Kekkonen's basic attitude has been more active. This is aptly reflected in a quotation in his book *Tamminiemi* ("A President's View") borrowed from the historian E.G. Palmén: "In order to save its position a small people must be able to produce clever initiatives to ward off dangers before they become too great".

It is in our interests to strive to influence developments in the world, wherever our fate is in the balance. A small country like Finland cannot express its desire for neutrality nowadays by withdrawing. We have no wish to become involved in great power disagreements in the sense of working for the interests of one power to the detriment of the other. This stance gives us the possibility to do our part in solving problems to the benefit of the entire international community. As President Kekkonen stated as long ago as 1960: "In matters of war and peace we are not neutral. We are on the side of a policy of peace and opposed to a policy of war."

The significance of Finland's active, peace-oriented policy of neutrality is in the results which it yields both to ourselves and to the entire international community. It is also on the basis of these results that our foreign policy is evaluated elsewhere in the world. We could not and do not ask for more.

The basic premise in our policy of neutrality is that we remain uninvolved in conflicts of interest between the superpowers. We see this both as being in accordance with the requirements of common sense and as enabling us, when the opportunity presents itself, to work for peaceful solutions acceptable to all involved. That is what we Finns mean when we describe our policy of neutrality as both active and peace-oriented.

Caution should not violate the interests of any outside party. Indeed, the opposite is the case. That is why it feels unpleasant when, perhaps due specifically to our caution, we are branded as "Finlandized" and presented as a cautionary example to others.

As far as I can see, the term "Finlandized" was created for use as a cudgel in contexts quite unrelated to Finnish foreign policy. That is why we consider its linkage with our country's name unjust. Every country formulates its own foreign policy and relations with other governments. That is just what Finland has done. We are not trying to thrust our line upon others, but we are glad to demonstrate our positive experiences to others, who may avail of them if they wish. We are proud of our achievements.

"Differences are not an obstacle, but rather a challenge," President Kekkonen stressed. The achievements which Finland has recorded in her stable relations with her neighbouring super-power, the Soviet Union, justify emphatic repetition of my predecessors's words. As a small nation, we Finns attach great importance to any peaceful international co-operation that creates security and welfare.

Finland takes an active part in international co-operation within the framework of her well-known and recognized policy of neutrality. This policy is an instrument that enables us to participate in the affairs of a changing world, and by means of it we have been able to produce the fruits of a realistic peace policy, enhancing both our own security and benefiting the international community. We shun anything that tends to exacerbate conflicts in international life and strive

85

to further understanding between states wherever the conditions for this exist.

Finland strives to safeguard her national security by pursuing an active, peace-oriented policy of neutrality based on good neighbourly relations.

An overridingly important precondition for the achievement of this goal is that all of our actions in the security-policy field enjoy international trust. Not only must our desire for peace be firm, but we must also have the ability to recognize and avert any violations of our territorial integrity with which we might be threatened.

Effective defence forces play their own part in ensuring the credibility of our security policy.

The maintenance and enhancement of this credibility is a matter for our various state bodies and all of our people.

Under the military provisions of the Treaty of Friendship, Co-operation and Mutual Assistance, Finland has pledged to defend herself, using all the forces available, in the event of an armed attack on her territory or, through Finland, the territory of the Soviet Union.

Thus Finland's defence of her own territory would occur within her own borders. As an independent state, she would defend herself in any event.

Any assistance provided by the Soviet Union to Finland would be agreed upon between our two countries.

By contrast, if the Soviet Union were to be attacked from any other quarter than through Finnish territory, the Treaty would not require any Finnish involvement in hostilities. Our aim is to do everything in our power to remain uninvolved in conflicts of interest between the superpowers, a right specifically enshrined in the preamble to the Treaty. Finland has consistently pursued this line in her foreign policy.

In the Paris Peace Treaty of 1947, Finland was prohibited from possessing, manufacturing or testing a number of weapons, including nuclear ones. In the early 1960s, she conducted negotiations with the signatory powers, foremost among them Great Britain and the Soviet Union, leading to agreement on her right to procure defensive missiles. And these have since been procured. We see this as a token of the trust enjoyed by our security policy.

Our security is mainly the fruit of means other than bolstering our military preparedness. That is why we have been very active in our efforts to preserve our good relations with neighbouring countries, and if possible to promote the improvement of relations between them as well. The global arms race is largely the result of insecurity and unrest. But on the other hand, the insecurity and unrest is also nurtured by the arms race. This vicious circle must be broken. That is why we worked very actively to ensure that the Madrid follow-up to the Conference on Security and Co-operation in Europe would be concluded with fruitful results. Our efforts elsewhere have had the same orientation.

We live in a world in which we are increasingly dependent on each other. The international situation has remained tense for several years now and there is no rapid turn for the better in sight. Finland, too, must ensure the all-round credibility of her security policy.

The most worrying feature is that the tensing of relations between the great powers has jeopardized the progress of disarmament negotiations. The pace of armament has been accelerating at the same time. For years, there have been so many nuclear weapons in the world that any belligerents could destroy each other with them many times over.

The effects of tension between the great powers have reached Europe, too. We hope that the superpowers will have the patience to continue and conclude negotiations concerning nuclear armaments in Europe. Safeguarding the CSCE process accords with the vital interests of Europe. Finland is doing everything in her power to strive for this goal.

Both alone and together with other neutral and nonaligned countries, Finland has presented numerous new initiatives aimed at strengthening security and developing co-operation in Europe. We are willing to present proposals in the future as well, provided we believe that they have a chance of being generally accepted. However, who it is that presents initiatives is not important, but rather that the development of co-operation already accomplished with so much effort is not allowed to be cut off.

8. Activity in Foreign Policy

A profile must be low, because otherwise it can not be raised if the need arises. A certain degree of caution is appropriate in the conduct of foreign affairs, but not passivity.

In a certain sense, Finland has always maintained a low profile, compared with others that one can see in the world. There was far greater activity in Urho Kekkonen's time than in Paasikivi's. But I see no point in activity just for the sake of being active. The decisive consideration should be how situations develop and what room exists for conspicuous actions or initiatives.

Our opportunities to influence the course of events are at their greatest when the great powers are willing to agree to strengthen peace. What we can do is present solution models and be available if we are needed. But if the superpowers do not possess the willingness that I have referred to, we must work with a longer-term perspective in the hope that better times will come.

Finland's success in her security policy presupposes correct assessments and conclusions in relation to the world situation, superpower relations, political relations in Europe and the situation in our immediate environment.

The fact that Finland has for so long been able to enjoy the benefits that come with a stable and peaceful international situation is something for which we can largely thank J.K. Paasikivi's and

Urho Kekkonen's ability to see clearly, in conducting foreign policy, what is essential in the international situation and what is of a transitory nature.

When Paasikivi and Kekkonen were beginning their tasks, the climate of opinion in Finland was essentially different from what it is today. Time and time again, they directed a serious appeal to the citizens and the media to recognize realities and behave with discretion.

I have not had to do that and hope that there will be no reason to do so in the future, either. By that I do not want to say that all of the stances taken in the media in relation to foreign powers with a friendly disposition towards us have always been within the limits of propriety.

Opinion polls conducted in recent years show indisputably that the overwhelming majority of the people have embraced the Paasikivi-Kekkonen Line as the natural and most advantageous foreign policy for us.

By force of circumstances, the formulation of questions in opinion polls is always rather simplified and on a very general plane. Therefore there is a need for continual analysis of our position in order to ensure that in the shadow of our great basic consensus we do not forget our basic premises and lose our ability attentively to follow the development of the international situation.

A foreign policy discussion of this kind,

intended as it is to be in the best interests of the people, is an essential part of Finnish democracy. However, it ought to be pointed out that those responsible for the management of foreign policy cannot engage in the discussion in the same way as private citizens. Where individuals responsible only for themselves can set forth their thoughts and express their feelings and moral condemnations, representatives of the State have to formulate the question in a different way.

When it takes decisions on stances and actions, the Government of Finland must assess how the various alternative decisions will influence the development of matters in the desired direction. Finland has placed the emphases in her foreign policy on maintaining good neighbourly relations, remaining aloof from conflicts between the great powers and promoting peaceful development everywhere. This corresponds with our national interests and its ethical justification cannot be questioned, either. The credible promotion of these goals requires deliberation and consistency.

I have nothing against academic discussion, which will not cause our line to waver one way or another. It would be a different matter if significant political groups were to question the basic premises of our foreign policy, but there is no evidence of that.

Discussion of foreign policy can today be

conducted with less emotion, since agreement exists on the basic solutions. This is in large measure the fruit of Urho Kekkonen's life work.

I also wish that statements concerning delicate matters involving our nation's foreign relations would not be issued at all possible times of the day and night.

Officials may amicably state views which are blameless in themselves, but which are nevertheless included in sensational articles. It can even happen that the newspaper in question builds up a particularly fierce attack against the person issuing the statement as a result of the view which he has presented in all good faith. What can we learn from this?

It would appear that a political discussion is going on in the guise of an academic discussion, but with academicism serving only as a fig leaf. It also appears that even what purports to be discussion is not really that, but rather squabbling about who dares to argue what.

According to the Constitution, the President of the Republic determines the State's relations with foreign powers. Although the same part of the constitution also contains provisions dealing with the role of Parliament in the management of foreign policy, the passage defining the status of the President has usually been emphasized in public discussion and the minds of the citizens. However, the sanction of Parliament is required for many treaties. The President can take decisions relating to war and peace only with the approval of Parliament. All notification to foreign powers or to representatives of Finland abroad must be made in co-operation with the Foreign Minister.

The relevant article in the Constitution is indeterminate in content and rather loosely expressed in that its phraseology as such does not enable one to conclude how the division of powers between the President of the Republic, the Council of State (Government) and Parliament in foreign affairs was originally intended to be.

It appears that when the Constitution was enacted there was no deeper deliberation of the details of decision making in the foreign-policy sphere; nor did its regulation become in any way a central question at the time. It would seem that the authority vested in the President to determine the State's relations with foreign states was not in a special position among his other powers.

On the other hand, it should be pointed out that entrusting the direction of foreign policy to the President in the new Constitution was in accord with those aspirations which were intended to create an independent position and extensive executive authority for the office.

The way in which power of decision has been exercised in external affairs has fluctuated in the period since Finland gained independence. Although even the early decades saw cases that emphasized the status of the head of state, only in the exceptional conditions of the 1940s does the conduct of foreign policy appear to have settled more obviously in his hands. In the course of recent decades, this tendency has strengthened and gradually consolidated itself.

Fluctuation in this exercise of power has been influenced both by prevailing circumstances and by the degree of interest in foreign-policy questions shown by the various incumbents of the presidency. And certainly not without significance, either, have been the opportunities that my two predecessors' long periods in office gave them to conduct a foreign policy guaranteeing long-term continuity. It cannot be disputed that the purposeful exercise of the head of state's powers in relation to foreign policy has been of benefit to our country in recent decades. It has helped our present foreign-policy line to be created and consolidated.

Meetings and the maintenance of contacts between national leaders nowadays hold a more central position in the management of foreign policy and international relations than they used to do. The study of international questions also requires more time and concentration than in earlier times. This naturally accentuates the position of that body of state which is considered to lead and thus, in the final analysis, to bear responsibility for foreign policy. In Finland, that means the Presidency.

It is clear and natural that both under the Constitution and in practice, the Council of State and, in particular, the Minister for Foreign Affairs and the cabinet foreign affairs committee play their important roles in foreign policy. The President must take his official decisions concerning this sphere at a meeting of the Council of State in the presence of parliamentarily responsible ministers, Parliament and its foreign relations committee likewise have their own tasks in this sphere.

Thus in our parliamentary system the management of foreign policy presupposes co-operation between the President, the Council of State and Parliament in forms that are appropriate and take our conditions into consideration. That, in my view, is the procedure to be followed, and it is adequately provided for in our Constitution.

It is important that each organ of state takes cognizance of its own sphere of competence and responsibility. Unclarities in the management of international relations will thus be avoided.

Depending on circumstances and within the limits set by our Constitution, the emphasis in the exercise of power can shift between different organs of state. In foreign policy, however, many facts and circumstances over which we have no control must be taken into consideration. These can lead to situations in which the President is forced to apply, more often than in other spheres, those constitutional provisions that give him independent powers of discretion and decision in matters within the scope of his authority.

For example, we can ask whether our situation is stable or unstable. Instability means that the centre of gravity is located too high. An unstable situation can be managed by a juggler with the skill to use the right amount of force at the right time. On the other hand, in a stable situation in which the centre of gravity is lower down, a considerable amount of force is needed to bring about any kind of change. I myself can recall a period in which an unstable situation was, so to speak, flipped over and righted by difficult ordeals. Now the new situation is considered natural and generally accepted. Only if a major East-West conflict erupts will we be in a difficult position. Where all other international conflicts are concerned, our location is an exceptional one. We are on the balcony, so to speak.

If one compares Finland's attitudes to international questions with those of, for example, Yugoslavia, it appears that both have made a virtue of necessity and got as much out of the situation as was to be had. Since Yugoslavia did not really have a European role to play, she turned to a reference group within a broader geographical context. Finland, too, has work to do in her own role, in such a way that it sets the tone for everything else. All of our endeavours are aimed overwhelmingly at being European and nothing more.

The Swedish author Gunnar Myrdal has said that anybody born in the Nordic countries has drawn the top prize in the lottery of life. Here on the periphery of things, we can watch, as though from a theatre box, what is going on in the world.

Our location has been exceptionally good if one examines the world as a whole, which has always been afflicted by conflicts; war and bloodshed. As I have said earlier, only a major clash between East and West can change that. But as long as common sense continues to have any place in the world, no such conflict will be unleashed.

Our destiny depends mainly on what happens in the world, but there are things that we can do as well. One goal worth striving for is a Nordic nuclear-weapons-free zone. It is not an alternative to disarmament, but it can to some degree enhance the security of the region.

It is easy to say that such matters are resolved only in big circles. But we are entitled to ask whether all things should always be settled in those circles. And we also have the answer: no, we must also have our say. Activity on our part also has the advantage that we have thought things through in preparation for the moment when the general preconditions for achieving solutions are better than they are today.

101

9. The Hopes of Peoples and Disarmament

The peoples of the world are justifiably worried. Finland, too, can continue to make an active contribution to promoting the improvement of international relations. That will naturally be easier to do if both great powers recognize a need to improve their relations.

There are indications that a new spiral in the arms race is beginning. The military alliances are presenting figures showing how their relative positions have been developing, and the other side's armament — or supposed armament — is used as justification for one's own armament schemes.

Since each of the superpowers already possesses more nuclear weapons than it needs to destroy the other completely, one can ask what it matters how many they have superfluous to requirements.

Until now, I have been of the opinion that nations should accomplish agreements providing for limitations and eventually reductions in armament levels. But if there is no prospect of such a development taking place, I feel that the only hope is that broad sections of the population will not follow their governments down that road. However, one cannot know what the consequences of such a course of development will be.

I see the greatest challenge of the decade as being that of warding off the dangers that nuclear weapons pose to humanity. Although there has long been an awareness of those dangers and although the inescapability of limiting armaments is recognized in principle everywhere, their number still continues to increase. Nevertheless, not a single nuclear weapon, no matter how efficient and devastating it may be, increases anybody's security.

The security of humanity can only be increased by taking concrete action to avert the danger of nuclear war and through mutual reductions in the numbers of nuclear weapons with the aim of universal and complete disarmament under an effective system of control.

It is fairly difficulty for an ordinary person to follow and understand questions relating to disarmament. If for instance, the great powers already have enough nuclear weapons to kill the population of the world ten times over, what is the point in trying to develop the ability to kill them an eleventh time?

One could also ask whether it matters so terribly much, given that the superpowers have quite enough destructive capability on a lower level as well, if they have the same levels of nuclear armament. However, when this question is asked, the answer is that it is unacceptable to have fewer arms than the other side, because the wrong conclusions might be drawn.

The nuclear powers' self-esteem, or at least their governments' conceptions of it, are somehow linked to their nuclear weapons, whose number and efficiency are considered to reflect national power.

On the other hand, many sensible people have noted that there is no rational way in which nuclear weapons can be used. The idea that they could be used in a limited context or on a small scale and then eschewed represents an extremely deceptive way of thinking. In practical terms, nuclear weapons can only have political significance, but never a military one.

More trust and good will must be created in the world. That is a precondition for the emergence of agreements between the great powers.

Peace movements have an important role of their own to play in this work. I believe that political decision-makers have begun to take more notice of these movements now that they include people who could not be considered radicals by any criterion whatsoever.

Nuclear weapons are first and foremost political weapons, without any actual military purpose. Unfortunately, this does not mean that there is no possibility or probability that they would ever be used. Of course, the governments of the nuclear powers behave with a sense of responsibility in relation to the fearsome arsenals that they posses. However, none of them has yet felt able to exclude the use of nuclear weapons under any circumstances.

Mankind has therefore been doomed to live

with the risk of nuclear war and with the fears that result from this. Our task in building security is to reduce the risk as much as possible. Assuming that nuclear weapons cannot be completely eliminated in the foreseeable future, the task is to find a situation where the desired political effects are achieved at the lowest possible level of armament and with the greatest possible downscaling of the risks inherent in their existence.

The nuclear stockpiles of the world have grown constantly ever since these weapons were invented. We seem to have reached a point where modern, deadly and destructive weapons are often manufactured, deployed and aimed at similar weapons belonging to the presumed opponent and then it is suggested that they will be withdrawn in exchange for corresponding measures on the other side. Nothing could better illustrate the existence of excess capability in the field of nuclear armament. It is obvious that this need to match and balance the capability of the rival or presumed adversary has a political basis that goes beyond rational calculation of military strength.

It follows from this that negotiations limited only to the field of arms control and disarmament are not sufficient. Much more is needed in order to bolster international security. There is an old argument about the relationship between improving political relations and disarmament: it is claimed on the one hand that better relations should make it easier to reach agreements on disarmament, but it is also said that agreements in the disarmament field contribute to better relations. Both arguments are probably correct, and efforts should be made in all areas at the same time. In my view, even modest and narrow agreements are politically helpful and encouraging.

Nuclear war is nowhere considered an instrument of rational policy. It would hardly be possible to limit such a war. Its effects would extend beyond all national boundaries. To order even the smallest nuclear strike as a reprisal measure in a crisis situation would quite probably lead to an all-out nuclear war. Awareness of this fact should lead to further agreements now. The use of force is prohibited by the UN Charter, but the peoples of the world are entitled to specific assurances against the use of nuclear weapons.

Finland has made her contribution by becoming a party to all treaties open to her in the disarmament sphere. In particular, she has consistently supported the Non-Proliferation Treaty as the best instrument to combat the spread of nuclear weapons, something that poses a threat to all states, nuclear and non-nuclear alike. We urge all nations to accede to the Treaty and to submit all of their activities in the nuclear field to international control. The availability and use of nuclear materials for peaceful purposes and preventing the proliferation of nuclear weapons are essentially complementary to each other.

By acceding to the Non-Proliferation Treaty, Finland has reaffirmed her commitment never to acquire nuclear weapons of her own. Nor do we allow any nuclear weapons on our territory. The non-nuclear status of Finland is thus comprehensive in the full meaning of the word. As a consequence, we are entitled to expect and to demand that such weapons are never, under any circumstances, used against us and that we are not threatened with them. We welcome the assurances given so far in this respect by the nuclear powers. We hope that they will eventually agree on a set of effective security guarantees.

Finland has sought to consolidate the existing nuclear-weapons-free status of the Nordic region by means of initiatives calling for the formalization of this status.

Opinion polls show that half of the American people believe that a major war will break out in the course of the present decade.

Thus people have an increasing sense of insecurity and express it in many ways. If we are to remain in touch with the prevailing facts, we must take note of this development of moods, which is just as much a reality as geographical and military conditions are.

The concern felt by the peoples of the world

stems from the way in which superpower relations and the world situation have tensed in recent years.

In fact, we must go back 20 years in time to arrive at a situation in which relations between the great powers were as inflamed as they are today.

However, it was specifically the Berlin and Cuban crises that provided the stimulus for serious practical measures aimed at détente and disarmament.

In the autumn of 1961, when the Berlin crisis was still making the peoples of Europe — including the Finns — live in fear of war, the Soviet and American UN ambassadors, Zorin and McCloy, issued a joint statement of principle, which has since been generally recognized as a decisive turning point in efforts to promote disarmament.

Their declaration did not achieve what it was actually intended to do, i.e. open the way to universal and complete disarmament under a system of international control. But it did loosen the logjam in American-Soviet negotiations and facilitated the work of the multilateral disarmament commission which had been set up in Geneva one year earlier.

The mechanism created two decades ago has continued to function in essentially the same way until the present day. The main emphasis remains on the two superpowers' efforts to achieve a concensus, although the negotiations are being formally conducted by the Geneva disarmament committee and the final agreement will be approved by the UN General Assembly.

The most important agreements accomplished in Geneva are the partial Test-Ban Treaty and the Non-Proliferation Treaty. The work of the Geneva committee has also led to the emergence of treaties banning the deployment of weapons of mass destruction in outer space and on the sea bed as well as the use of biological weapons and environmental warfare.

The last-mentioned treaty came about in 1977, since which negotiations aimed at a total ban on chemical weapons and nuclear tests have been bogged down.

The Cuban Crisis in the autumn of 1962 forced the Soviet Union and the United States to give serious consideration to effective measures to prevent nuclear war. However, it still took seven years before the situation was ripe for the Strategic Arms Limitation Talks (SALT), which began in Helsinki in 1969. Both sides were prepared to recognize that increasing the number of nuclear weapons did not enhance security, since each side had the ability to destroy the other in any case.

The real impetus came from their mutual need to prevent the development of anti-missile technology, which was seen as a threat to the established balance of terror. It is paradoxical that this

112

weapons system, on the face of it a defensive one, was seen as increasing the danger of war, whereas a mutually assured retaliatory capacity was considered to safeguard equilibrium and security.

This philosophy of mutually assured destruction (MAD) was confirmed in the first SALT agreements, which were signed in 1972.

Anti-missile systems were limited to a minimal level and quantitative restrictions imposed on strategic missiles armed with nuclear warheads.

In practice, SALT meant arms control, not disarmament. It did not stop technological development, nor even growth in the number of nuclear weapons. Due mainly to technological development, above all the introduction of MIRVed (multiple-warhead) missiles, the number of nuclear warheads in the superpowers' arsenals has increased several-fold since the early 1970s.

The purpose of the SALT II agreement was to halt this quantitative growth more permanently and to impose some technological limitations as well. However, as we well know, this agreement has still not been ratified.

Today's unrest in the world is doubtlessly due in part to the fact that nuclear weapons continue to be modernized and deployed beyond any reasonable need.

People's refusal to submit to a new acceleration in the arms race has been a decisive factor in the refusal of détente to die, here in Europe at least.

Ordinary people and the organizations to which they belong have rallied to oppose a return to the Cold War and the increasing threat of a nuclear catastrophe.

The debate on the deployment of nuclear weapons in Europe and the proposed Nordic nuclear-weapons-free zone is an indication that public opinion in support of peace has become a significantly influential reality in superpower politics as well.

Political institutions, and in particular political parties, must take this new positive phenomenon into account. Indeed, they must be able to do even more; they must be able to build a bridge between public opinion and political dicision making, between slogans and practical détente.

One of the great weaknesses in the process of détente that began in the early 1960s was obviously that it relied more on diplomatic negotiations than on the active support of large segments of the population.

A mobilization of public opinion in recent years presages a new and more vital coming of détente.

We are living in a period of major uncertainty in international politics. I can not but note with concern that our continent is beset by new kinds of concerns and difficulties. Many profound economic, societal and political change factors are putting our ability to maintain peaceful development in Europe to the test. Security is being sought on an ever-higher level of armament at the same time as results from negotiations concerning arms reductions still fail to manifest themselves. Awareness of the unprecedented military destructive power concentrated in Europe as well as of the inescapable community of destiny to which all parts of Europe belong inevitably prompts a sense of insecurity.

However, security is an incomparably broader concept than merely problems concerned with the danger of war. It includes expectations relating to people's conditions of livelihood, societal development and interaction in a broader sense; striving for a better and more just tomorrow. That is why, in the final analysis, it is only close rapprochement between the peoples of Europe and open co-operation to promote mutual trust that can guarantee the permanence of this state of peace in our continent.

It is precisely with the aim of promoting progress towards these goals that the work of the Conference on Security and Co-operation in Europe has been going on for more than a decade. The long-term goals, which are set forth in the document bearing Helsinki's name, the Final Act, express the shared will of the 35 participating states to create deeper trust and more open interaction in Europe as well as a process of development aimed at co-operation beneficial to all.

It must be admitted that the achievement of the

mutually agreed goals has proved more difficult than was perhaps anticipated. It may also be that the tension that has tainted international relations in recent years has accentuated difficulties and undermined efforts towards progress along the road staked out in the Final Act. That notwithstanding, we Finns believe that the process remains essentially vital, because it is based on the permanent and real interests of all the 35 countries involved. I consider it important that in the minds of the people it becomes a living and effective process, so that its goals — security and co-operation — are perceived as worth constantly striving for.

We are concerned about the international climate and its future development. This concern is undoubtedly shared with us by all peoples, whose basic interests are the preservation of peace and balanced development towards a better world.

In the present situation it is very important that we do not allow our anxiety to develop into fruitless pessimism or fatalism. It cannot be disputed that in the final analysis the superpowers are the decisive factor when decisions are being taken. But experience has shown that small and medium-sized states can influence international developments even in an unfavourable international climate.

This spirit and the realistic premise that there

is no other alternative for our continent than the preservation of peace and mutual co-operation find practical expression with particular clarity in the way in which we have worked together for the Conference on Security and Co-operation in Europe.

The importance of co-operation between the neutral and nonaligned countries of Europe is acknowledged within the CSCE process, where the services of countries outside the power blocs are needed.

The process of implementation of the Helsinki Final Act has produced substantial benefits. It has brought about a lasting improvement in the situation, a fact that is relevant to the security of all nations in Europe and the well-being of individuals. This must not be forgotten, however slow — and even frustrating — the ongoing process may sometimes appear.

We see it as a learning process. Humanity will have to learn to solve or manage international problems peacefully and through negotiation in this era of extremely destructive weapon systems. A high level of military preparedness in Europe and the scale of nuclear armament cause constant unease in the minds of people in Finland.

In many respects, however, Finland's position is good. In Scandinavia or the Nordic region there is no suspicious atmosphere of confrontation, no nuclear weapons, and mutual co-operation is well developed. The region is stable and peaceful, but the situation is sensitive. The superpowers and military alliances are showing a growing interest in the region. We are certain that it is in everybody's interests that tension here be kept at a low level.

What is needed now is the building of mutual trust. If one takes the attitude that international agreements have no value to speak of, because they have been broken in the past, the prospects for the future are quite bleak. The alternative to negotiation and agreements is obviously an arms race fuelled by mistrust and mistrust fuelled by the arms race.

Finland is working to oppose apartheid and takes the view that the UN and its Security Council should undertake additional action in this matter. We urge constant international support for the Frontline States and liberation movements in Southern Africa.

The international community is constantly concerned about the situation in Namibia. Finland, which has long been a member of the UN's Council on Namibia and has had friendly relations with the Namibian people for over a century, is closely interested in that country achieving independence soon. The people of Namibia must be given their inaliable right to self-determination. The Government of Finland hopes to see rapid progress towards independence through implementation, without delay and effectively, of the Security Council's Resolution 435.

10. Economic Relations

The instability that has plagued the international currency system since the 1970s does not appear to be so much an indication of weakness in the system itself as of rapid change in real factors that affect the world economy. Disparities between the development of different countries' inflation rates and balances of payment have made the basis on which currencies rest a very unsteady one. Under those circumstances, it has probably been a good thing all round that the currency and payments systems have been flexible and capable of making room for change.

Of course, if general economic uncertainty continues too long, there is the danger that the currency system will come under too much pressure. Such a danger could arise if, for instance, the acute debt problem afflicting developing countries and some of the industrial countries as well can not be coped with in an organized manner.

Not even a crisis in the banking system can be completely ruled out. One could be caused by debtor countries going bankrupt or by excessive tightening of international credits due to cautiousness on the part of banks. It is to be hoped that the authorities will be able to create, through the International Monetary Fund and the Bank for International Settlements, the security system needed to avert this danger.

One proof of the flexibility with which the system has developed is the clear movement of the International Monetary Fund away from the "policing" role that it performed in relation to currencies in the 1950s and 1960s to its current character as a co-operative organization and financial institution, which has been able in many ways to assist its member countries to adapt in the face of their economic difficulties. From the perspective of the system, it is important that the conditions in which the IMF must work be safeguarded, e.g. through ensuring that increases in its capital are effected without delay.

Prior to 1974, a good IMF member kept its balance of payments in balance. In the event of any disturbance in external equilibrium, the country tried, with the IMF's support, to restore it.

However, a strong rise in the price of oil gave the oilexporting countries an unprecedentedly large collective balance of payments surplus, and a corresponding deficit had to show itself somewhere else. Now a good member was one that incurred its share of the inevitable deficits and refrained from too strictly and selfishly trying to maintain equilibrium in its balance of payments.

The industrial countries did indeed succeed in eliminating their own balance of payments deficit in relation to the oil exporters within a few years, but in the case of the developing countries deficits became a pretty permanent phenomenon. In these altered conditions, the IMF's loan conditions became problematic. Viewed from the perspective of an international organization, it is always difficult to determine what would be a wise policy for a member country to pursue. It can easily come about that the economic thinking prevailing in developed countries sets the tone.

The developing countries have been advocating an increase in the IMF's equity capital, which would enable all member countries to improve their liquidity without conditions. That is because members are entitled to withdraw part of the equity capital fairly automatically. By contrast, the more developed industrial countries have wanted to maintain the very far-reaching conditions currently applied.

The developing countries are demanding an increase in special drawing rights as a condition for a linkage between them and development aid. By doing so, they have merely succeeded in hindering such an increase, but have failed to prevent the missing special drawing rights from being replaced by an increase in the numbers of US dollars in the currency reserves of countries all over the world.

Private international financial institutions have to a very considerable extent financed the inevitable deficits by accepting fairly short-term deposits from countries with surpluses and using them to grant longer-term credits to those with deficits. Since more and more countries have drifted or are drifting into insolvency, the IMF has had to act as a kind of pilot, which guides lending by private banks and gives its blessing to the policy pursued.

Sudden upward and downward shifts in exchange rates, due sometimes to differences between interest rates and sometimes to psychological factors or longer-term economic development trends, can not, unfortunately, be avoided as long as both large surpluses and the corresponding large deficits exist. Currencies can be stable only as long as economies are stable.

Finland's trade policy situation became problematic in the early 1970s. In conditions made very difficult by simultaneous negotiations on the German question and the status of Berlin, she had to take a position on the market-integration solutions then being implemented in Western Europe. From her point of view, the outcome was positive insofar as she did not end up the losing party.

The big question of the 1960s was whether or not the European Economic Community would be enlarged. Prospects were on occasion very threatening, negotiations with the countries seeking accession having failed as yet to yield results and those between the EEC and EFTA countries still being in progress. Measured by commercial criteria, Finland's agreement with the EEC was as good from her point of view as was possible in that situation. In every respect but the wood-processing industry, Finland was a marginal factor to the EEC.

Then, when Finland, for the sake of balance, signed a series of agreements lowering barriers to

trade with the members, other than the Soviet
Union, of the Council for Mutual Economic
Assistance, I feared that there would be a reaction
on the part of third countries. Would they argue
that these agreements were contrary to what we
had agreed on in GATT? This question of
preference was slightly problematic, and President
Kekkonen was very instrumental in solving it,
although even he hardly knew in advance how to go
about it.

For all their complexity, the negotiations led to a
happy outcome from Finland's point of view. The
most important achievement was the fact that
Finland did not find herself behind a tariff barrier
and growing obstacles to trade in the West. Indeed,
barriers to trade were slightly lowered in the West
and in the East Finland was able to retain the
benefits that she had enjoyed.

Trade between Finland and the Soviet Union rests
on a solid basis of agreements. As early as 1947 the
two countries agreed to grant each other most-
favoured-nation status, and on this basis have
gradually proceeded to what amounts in practice to
free trade in industrial products. Since the same
year, our trade has been conducted on a system of
clearing payments. The guiding principle from the
very beginning has been that trade must be
beneficial to both partners. These principles, which
have already become traditions, as well as the basic
endeavour constantly to develop our trade relations,

which is confirmed in the Treaty of Friendship, Co-operation and Mutual Assistance, have proved sound, enduring and fruitful in practice. It is perhaps the bilateral character of our trade that has enabled the Finnish business sector to be involved on such a really broad front. This involvement has also been substantially encouraged by the five-year outline agreements concluded since 1951. The main outlines that our co-operation in the economic, scientific and technological spheres would follow far into the future were given shape in a long-term programme signed in 1977 and now extended to cover the period up to 1995.

It has been clearly evident in recent years that the importance of protocols coverning visible trade has been accentuated as factors in our overall trade. Using them, we actively strive towards our common goal: balanced trade at as high a volume as possible. We also try to take account of two additional goals: the prevention of strong sectoral fluctuations and structural diversification of Finnish imports.

We are convinced that our imports from the Soviet Union are of major importance in many respects. They have in the past enabled us to reduce the detrimental effects of various international crises on our economy. We shall bear that in mind in our future planning as well. At the same time as we are striving to promote demand for imported Soviet goods in Finland, we trust that the Soviet Union's export range will continue to grow and diversify.

The course of development that the world will probably follow is one in which the development of research, control and technology will see the industrial countries depending to some extent or other on nuclear power to generate electricity. Today, however, it is impossible to forecast with any certainty how the technological challenges of the next millenium will be answered. We can only conclude that continuing growth in the production of goods will greatly depend on those technological solutions.

Here in Finland we are still in the enviable situation that within our reach are a whole range of electricity generation alternatives based on both indigenous and imported energy. Our oil imports are based on bilateral trade, which gives us certain growth- and employment-related advantages over many other countries. Therefore, it would appear that cautious and well-considered monitoring of world developments would accord well with our domestic energy policy.

Technological development in recent decades has shrunk the world so much that today our neighbours are not just the peoples living across our borders. Famine and crises in the Third World affect us and our welfare in the same way as the problems of the Baltic region affected us in Snellman's days a century ago.

That means that we can not isolate ourselves in implementing our foreign policy, but must pursue a well-considered, peace-oriented policy of neutrality, striving consistently for détente and a sharing of responsibility in the face of accumulating problems of development.

The young, in particular, have understood this, and significant popular movements for peace, development and a better environment have sprung up in Finland, as elsewhere. The popular activism for peace that has awakened in various countries is one of the few hope-inspiring signs that we have seen in these grave times.

During the presidential election campaign in 1982, there were fairly unanimous calls for an increase in Finland's official aid to developing countries. It seems obvious that development cooperation will have an increasingly central role in the work of future governments. In periods of slow economic growth, this will naturally mean that there will be relatively limited scope for increases in funds earmarked for our own purposes.

In our societal policy in general, we shall have to allow more room for efforts to improve the quality of life and emphasize the significance of non-economic factors. More resources will have to be allocated to environmental protection and occupational safety. There will have to be increased efforts to stimulate people's work motivation and alleviate new alienation phenomena. Life must be given a content and the purpose of helping nations poorer than ourselves.

Programmes are continually being approved by the UN, but in general have not been implemented. There is so much selfishness that nobody wants to transfer the necessary resources. People feel a strong need to raise their own standard of living.

Everybody can make his or her own practical contribution to development work, but I have noticed that many are more willing to do so in theory than in practice.

If a country's balance of payments is in deficit and debts are incurred in order to cover the funds channelled into development aid, what this means in practice is that the aid is left for future generations to pay. There must be a willingness to accept the real burdens that giving development aid involves. It seems that this willingness exists on an increasing scale in Finland.

Something that I can not condone at all is that the same people demand both an increase in development aid and growth in the national debt. It appears that they have not properly understood that more aid also means some burdens and some sacrifices. Increasing foreign borrowing to finance development aid is hardly a form of generosity, since it merely means passing on the bill to our children.

I have expressed my concern at our apparently greater willingness to participate in principle than to make sacrifices in practice. Of course the easiest way out is to criticize the superpowers. If one starts from the premise that they should act, but do not, one can easily believe that one need not do anything oneself. And one can pick up a few points for sympathy in the process.

Moralizing and development aid, i.e. giving it, suit each other well. But when we begin any deeper deliberation of whom it should be given to and discussing what conditions the recipient country should fulfill, we run into considerable difficulties. It is quite obvious that the overwhelming majority of UN member countries are either under military rule or in any event ruled in a way that deprives their citizens of any influence over their rulers. There are very few countries to which development aid could be given in accordance with principles that all of us have accepted.

We should donate development aid unselfishly, but obviousсly it will become quite a burden on us. Therefore, we should try to make our donations in such a way that the burden on us is less, from the viewpoints of our economy and employment, than it would be if we made them in a purely charitable manner.

The world population is now about 4,400 million, and is forecast to increase to 6,300 million or so by the end of the century. By far the greatest part of this increase will be in developing countries. Their foodstuffs production will have to more than double if the needs caused by population growth are to be

132

satisfied and nutrition levels raised. A production increase of this magnitude will demand very strong efforts, because most developing countries have become major importers of agricultural commodities in recent decades.

Hunger can be permanently eradicated only by boosting the developing countries' own foodstuffs production. In the final analysis, the responsibility for this resides with those countries themselves, but also the industrial countries must do everything in their power to support poor countries' efforts to develop their agriculture.

Finland is a well-off member of the international community. We, too, must play our part in the struggle against hunger and malnutrition by meeting our general commitments with respect to development aid. We possess a considerable fund of agricultural expertise, which can be availed of in many ways.

I really do think that East-West trade and other similar activities, besides directly alleviating grave economic problems that the world is facing today, could be a valuable factor in building confidence and easing international tensions. There is abundant evidence of how mutually beneficial economic relations have contributed to improving the international climate. This has been the case throughout history and not just in East-West matters. Moreover, it seems to me that whenever trade becomes a factor subjected to aims alien to its own internal dynamics, it tends to sharpen potential tensions of political origin.

Finland, like most small and medium-sized countries, relies heavily on foreign trade. That is why we cannot really welcome any measures which would curtail economic interaction between states.

I should also think that commercial intercourse between East and West might play an active role in bringing people closer to each other, different sociopolitical approaches notwithstanding, and eliminate unnecessary misunderstanding between them. This is also very much in line with our general standpoint at the Conference on Security and Co-operation in Europe.

If trade helps to bring about substantial and lasting welfare, it is not worth while for anybody to risk it through confrontations of a political nature. If that is what is meant by interdependence, I am certainly a supporter of it.

11. Distorted Conceptions of Good Neighbourly Relations

The use of the word "Finlandization" does not do justice to Finland in any way. Its use does not mean that something has happened in Finland. It is somewhere else that something happens, and it is in a debate conducted elsewhere that one wants to use the term. If one thinks of Finland's development, one can ask whether her policy of friendship or anything else has weakened her position. When she had just fought two wars against the Soviet Union and then, in the autumn of 1944, had to begin expelling German forces from the northern parts of her territory, her position as a state was not particularly strong. However, it was in that situation that she began the work of building up her present status, which is internationally recognized and, in the view of the overwhelming majority of her citizens, good and strong. We are able to participate in the life of the international community, as a fully-fledged member of that community.

But when our country's name is used as a cudgel with the intention of causing pain to those struck, those who use it obviously never realize that also the cudgel can have feelings. If our country is used as a bludgeon — and, as we see it, entirely unjustifiably — it naturally upsets us, and we would prefer if some more appropriate words could be found instead of misusing Finland's name.

Finlandization is talked of in various parts of the

world from time to time, although none of our behaviour has provided any justification for it. The aim has been to present Finland as a cautionary example of a country that has eschewed its independence in order to appease a large neighbour.

Our reply to that is that Finland has not given up any of her interests for the sake of good neighbourly relations. It is in her interests to pursue a policy of peace and neighbourliness in her relations with her neighbouring countries.

What it boils down to is that people want to use our country's name for purposes that have nothing to do with us.

That being the case, and since it recurs every now and then, the matter is not worth getting upset about, nor is there any point in issuing indignant protests in an effort to make those who use the term change their tune. They do not know our country and if, for some reason or other, they feel justified in using its name for their own purposes, we can not make them come round to our point of view. There is no point in replying to their utterances day after day, as recently happened after the American General Roger's impertinent statement, in which he doubted the preparedness of the Finns to protect their territorial inviolability.

It is obvious that world events are criticized less in Finland than, for example, in Sweden. It could be said that in our statements we have adopted and continue to adopt a lower profile. When something new happens, when issues are still fresh, the Finnish state and its leaders usually react. But we have tried to be pragmatic and to put forward proposals and ideas that have a chance of leading to results. However, it is not very often that we have been able to make a contribution to increasing international understanding. Nevertheless, our role in promoting the idea of European co-operation and in hosting the Conference on Security and Co-operation in Europe can certainly be attributed in part to our good relations with all states.

There is a free press in Finland and we hope that it deals with other countries' affairs objectively and informatively and not emotionally. There have also been some features that can not be considered high-class, but they have in no way damaged our good relations with other countries.

There has been much talk in the world about Finlandization. I have tried to understand what people actually mean when they use the expression. Perhaps they think that our position has deteriorated during the past few years; that because of our friendly relations with the Soviet Union we have lost something in our international position that we had before.

We have gone through two wars, but neither of them led to our being occupied. One can often read in Western accounts of those wars that Finland surrendered, but that is simply not true. We lost the war and signed a peace treaty, and then later, in 1948, a treaty with the Soviet Union which has prompted quite a lot of interest. It was very much in Finland's interests to accomplish such a treaty, and the basic principles of our foreign policy have been based on its preamble ever since. It includes Finland's right to remain aloof from the great powers' conflicts of interest. There was once much suspicion, and even hatred, between Finland and the Soviet Union, but we have learnt to live together with peoples who are and will remain our neighbours. Our feelings are now based on friendship, mutual understanding and shared interests. The Soviets and ourselves are now good neighbours to each other. If they have problems elsewhere, it does not mean that we have problems here. One could even say that the opposite is the case. When they have problems elsewhere, we — and they — understand even better how precious it is for a country to have good neighbours and to be free of unresolved problems with them. We simply want to increase trade and expand relations with them. We want to maintain good relations with the Soviet Union.

It is natural that problems will crop up if the level of tension in the world rises and mistrust increases, especially if that happens between our neighbours. In such an event, we shall have every reason to be concerned, but we believe that our mutual relations need not suffer from it in any way.

The term "Finlandization" has quite frequently been used by some foreign writers and commentators. In most cases this term has been used in contexts which have no reference to Finland or her politics. Of course, we in Finland do not like this term, because it gives a completely distorted idea about our country and the foreign policy, which we have chosen in accordance with our national interests. Therefore we would like to see it dropped from the political vocabulary.

The term "Finlandization" often crops up in political usage and nobody in Finland wants to hear it. If that concept referred to the relationship based on equality and mutual respect prevailing between a small and a large state having different social systems, we would not object to it. However, as it is being used as a striking weapon in entirely different contexts, we are, naturally, not happy about it.

12. Facing the Future

It would be interesting to know whether Paasi-kivi was really the pessimist that his statements would lead one to believe. An opinion that has been voiced about economic forecasts is that they are presented not in the belief that they will prove correct, but that they will prove incorrect. That would mean that they have a pedagogic aspect. If that is the case, one must ask to what extent Paasi-kivi felt a need to focus attention on what could happen; what is possible. It is difficult to believe that he could have been as pessimistic as many of his statements made him sound. He clearly had faith in the future, just as though he did not believe that the situation was always as bad as it looked. Thus if a situation is described as very bad, expectations are forced downwards, and the prospects for success are perhaps better than when a very optimistic picture is painted and the result is disappointment.

Finland's international political position is stable. This has been greatly influenced by the life-long efforts of my honoured predecessors J.K. Paasikivi and Urho Kekkonen. I do not intend to spoil the heritage, nor will I allow it to be spoiled.

We are not threatened by anyone, nor do we threaten anyone in any way.

When I took the oath of office before Parliament, I did not believe it would be very difficult to convince the outside world of the permanence of our foreign policy lines. After all, the vast majority of the Finnish people and all Finland's noteworthy political forces are unanimous on this point.

The difficulty has not been to convince the governments of foreign states. This has been made unequivocally clear during the visits which I have been able to pay to the Soviet Union and Sweden in this short time. The same is true of the discussions which I had with the President of France.

On the other hand, the foreign press has claimed to see changes, although on the day I took office I assured its representatives that "Finland will continue without wavering on the path marked by my two predecessors".

I wish to stress quite emphatically that the basic principles of our foreign policy are unchanged, nor will they change during my term of office.

As in most other countries, the UN's Disarmament Week is observed in Finland. Tens of thousands of young people work actively for peace and disarmament. They come out in support of our foreign-policy principles and our government's initiatives in the cause of détente.

Young people are naturally critical and would like the authorities to be more active in relation to many matters than they now are. That is the way young people are. It demonstrates their alertness in relation to societal matters and their desire to participate in the democratic system.

In many respects, young people have better prospects in life than had the generation to which I belong. In particular where the expansion of educational opportunities is concerned, there has been a very considerable change for the better in Finland in recent decades. However, structural unemployment has threateningly reduced their chances of finding jobs. The greatest tasks that Finnish society will have to take care of in this decade are the elimination of youth unemployment and ensuring that the generation now growing up has a future to look forward to.

The peoples of the world are clearly losing their faith that the level of armaments could fall again after the recent rearmament decisions and disarmament negotiations.

The hope of peoples is in the peoples themselves.

Many of the most serious threats to international security today unfortunately seem to be beyond the reach of the United Nations. The use of force in international relations has remained a regrettably common phenomenon. This is one of the principal challenges to the authority of the United Nations.

The United Nations must be strengthened. A strong UN is in the interests of both its small and large members. The parties involved in international disputes often forget this. Such an

147

attitude to the UN is based on short-sighted calculations and political expediency, and the results are tragic for everybody concerned.

The world can ill afford such a development. To counteract it, we must look realistically at the facilities allowed the principal United Nations bodies.

The Security Council bears primary responsibility for international peace and security. The implementation and observance of Security Council resolutions by member states are the cornerstone of the Charter and the foundation on which the viability of the United Nations rests as a whole. Yet the heaviest responsibility falls on the permanent members of the Security Council. Their failure to agree on a specific dispute in no way absolves them or the Council from the obligations imposed on them by the Charter.

The international community, in particular small states like Finland, will always look to the Security Council for swift and decisive action to impose its will, to stop aggression and to promote the peaceful settlement of disputes. This has often proved impossible. States have learned that the United Nations does not guarantee their security. Instead one should learn that the task of the United Nations is not only to stop wars but to prevent them.

The UN could be the most effective instrument of preventive action. Member countries should avail fully of the services that the organization can offer in achieving and maintaining peace. That is the way to a sensible world order in accordance with the Charter.

The Charter remains as valid as ever, but the working methods and procedures of the principal UN bodies may need adaptation on the basis of experience. Above all, this concerns the functioning of the Security Council, which we hope will be able to develop procedures for initiating action in the early stage of conflicts in order to prevent the use of force.

Preventive diplomacy and inhibiting the use of force are challenges both to the Security Council and to the whole international community. All countries live in the shadow of nuclear weapons, and nothing can be more important than preventing nuclear war. Tension between nuclear powers is therefore a source of concern to all.

Environmental protection is today recognized as an important task in international co-operation. Indeed, it is one of the cornerstones of a common strategy for the survival of humanity. If they are to be able to live in harmony with each other, people must learn to live in harmony with nature. Environmental protection and peace are inseparably interwoven values.

The signing of the Helsinki Convention on prevention of pollution in the Baltic in 1974 indicated that the states around the sea were ready to recognize its importance in enhancing the quality of life in the whole region. The agreement was accomplished in less than a year, an astonishingly brief period when one considers what pioneering work was involved.

The Convention is unique and innovative in that it is the first international agreement which takes into account all factors with a polluting impact on the marine environment. The Baltic can be considered a kind of testing ground, where events — be they successes or failures — will be closely followed by the whole world. If the parties to it succeed in arresting the pollution of the Baltic through the Convention itself and related national measures, they will have created a new and exemplary environmental policy that will be of growing importance in the future.

The Convention has already served as a model in negotiating other agreements coverning the protection of the marine environment in various parts of the world.

Both the Helsinki Convention and the 1973 Gdansk Convention, which covered fishing and the protection of biological natural resources in the Baltic and the straits leading to the North Sea, were pioneering in another respect as well. They were the first regional agreements to include all of the Baltic's littoral states. Thus they served as a dress rehearsal for the Conference on Security and Co-operation in Europe, which was brought to a successful conclusion only a little later, in 1975.

I hope that Finland in the year 2000 will be a country that keeps out of world headlines. We shall look after our own business, and if we have the resources to help others, well and good. The most important thing is that we do not become a burden on others.

References

HISTORICAL NOTES

FUNDAMENTAL INTERESTS

A POLICY OF GOOD NEIGHBOURLY RELATIONS

FINLAND AND THE SOVIET UNION

A PEACE-ORIENTED POLICY OF NEUTRALITY

ACTIVITY IN FOREIGN POLICY

THE HOPES OF PEOPLES AND DISARMAMENT

ECONOMIC RELATIONS

DISTORTED CONCEPTIONS OF GOOD NEIGHBOURLY RELATIONS

FACING THE FUTURE